# Walking

*the*

# Mystical Path

*of*

# Jesus

From the Heart of Jesus, vol 2

# Walking

*the*

# Mystical Path

*of*

# Jesus

KIM MICHAELS

MORE TO LIFE PUBLISHING

www.morepublish.com

For foreign and translation rights,

contact info@morepublish.com

ISBN: 978-9949-518-25-8

Series ISBN: 978-9949-518-21-0

The information and insights in this book should not be considered as a form of therapy, advice, direction, diagnosis, and/or treatment of any kind. This information is not a substitute for medical, psychological, or other professional advice, counseling and care. All matters pertaining to your individual health should be supervised by a physician or appropriate health-care practitioner. No guarantee is made by the author or the publisher that the practices described in this book will yield successful results for anyone at any time. They are presented for informational purposes only, as the practice and proof rests with the individual.

For more information: www.askrealjesus.com.

# CONTENTS

# INTRODUCTION | THERE MUST BE MORE TO LIFE!

During my childhood and teen-age years, I knew something was missing from my life. I always sensed that there simply had to be more to life than what I was experiencing. There had to be a better, richer, more fulfilling way of life than what I was observing in the lives of the adults around me and in my society.

At the age of 18, I discovered the missing ingredient and began to understand – at least in part – who I am and why I am here. I found a book that opened up an entirely new world to me, a world that I had sensed but never seen. What I discovered was that the material world is like the tip of an iceberg, and it is part of a larger whole, of which 90 percent is hidden from our physical senses. You might think that what I am talking about here is religion. After all, most of the world's religions talk about a spiritual world that we cannot see. Yet I was never interested in what is normally called religion. I was repulsed by mainstream religion because even though it talks about the spiritual world, it is still missing the essential ingredient. The X-factor I was looking for simply wasn't there in mainstream religion.

The ingredient that was missing from my life, and from most religions, is the concept of a spiritual path, a mystical path. It was this path that I discovered at the age of 18, and I have been following the path ever since, now for over 30 years. I see this path as a systematic process whereby we can increase our understanding of the spiritual world and this world. We can gain a deeper understanding of who we are, who God is and why we are here on this beautiful, but somewhat treacherous, little planet.

As we increase our understanding of who we are, we can begin to interact with the spiritual world. We can have a variety of mystical experiences that show us the reality of the spiritual world. Eventually, such experiences can help us integrate with the spiritual world and with a part of ourselves that is permanently residing in that world. We can begin to build a new sense of identity, and we will come to understand and accept that we are not simply mortal, limited human beings who are condemned to a life of suffering. We can realize that life is not a meaningless game of chance and that we are not simply victims of circumstances beyond our control. Instead, we have the potential to take command over ourselves, our lives and our world—and this is a big part of our purpose for being here.

## A richer life

After I discovered the mystical path, my life took on a richer sense of meaning and direction. I have come to understand who I am, I know my personal mission in life and I know where I am going. The contrast between this spiritual lifestyle and the purposeless and materialistic lifestyle is dramatic and for me all-important. After experiencing how much more fulfilling life can be when you follow the inner path, I developed a deep desire to share this knowledge with other people.

That desire became very strong shortly after I discovered the path, and I directed it toward my non-religious family. At a memorable dinner party, I tried to share my enthusiasm for the spiritual path and was met with an impenetrable wall of suspicion and resistance. This was partly my responsibility because I was thinking that if only all other people would accept my beliefs, we could surely solve all of the world's problems. Nevertheless, the experience taught me that many people are simply not ready for the path and have no interest in it whatsoever. To my surprise, I have found that this is even true for many religious people. They are open to their particular religion, but they are not interested in hearing about a universal path that transcends all outer religions.

Fortunately, I also discovered that a smaller, but rapidly growing, number of people are ready to hear about the mystical path, and they will recognize the validity of the path—if it is described in terms they can understand and accept. Most of these people have been brought up in a culture that is a battleground between materialistic science and orthodox Christianity – both of which deny the existence of a spiritual path – and they simply do not understand what they are looking for. Although many of these people are suspicious of materialism, they are nevertheless also suspicious of traditional religions. They need a description of the path that is truly universal and does not require them to shave their heads or yell "Jeeesus!" with exalted voices. This book will provide such a universal description.

## Why do we need Jesus?

I am aware that some readers will have questions about the claim that this book is the result of a conversation with the spiritual being who was embodied as Jesus. Yet allow me to give you a few thoughts to ponder. I personally rejected the image of Jesus that was presented to me by the Lutheran church. I simply could not relate to that Jesus, and consequently I could not accept him as a spiritual teacher. The book that introduced me to the spiritual path also gave me a thought that eventually changed my view of Jesus. The thought was that over the course of history, Jesus' original message has been distorted for a variety of political reasons. This made me realize that perhaps there was a deeper, more universal, side of Jesus than what is presented by orthodox Christianity.

The key idea concerning the mystical path is that there is a spiritual world that exists alongside the material world. We are the self-conscious beings living in the material world, and there are also self-conscious beings in the spiritual world. Some of these spiritual beings, or masters, have volunteered to serve as our spiritual teachers. Their task is to help us become who we really are. As part of this work, our spiritual teachers have given us numerous teachings. Some of them have been turned into orthodox, sectarian, exclusivist religions, as has certainly happened to the Christian religion. Yet this was not the original intent of our spiritual teachers. They have always been trying to help us discover the universal path that transcends all man-made, dualistic divisions. The essence of this path is that we have the potential to raise our consciousness and thereby become the spiritual beings on earth that we already are in a higher realm.

When I began to understand the concept of spiritual masters, I realized that Jesus is today such a master. I also began to understand that Jesus did not come to start another sectarian religion that would become as closed-minded as the Jewish religion that killed him. He came to teach and demonstrate a universal path to a higher state of consciousness, and I began to see Jesus as a universal spiritual teacher. Scholars have discovered that the early followers of Jesus were not called "Christians" but "Followers of the Way."

The idea that Jesus is a universal spiritual teacher was much more acceptable to me than the idolized image presented by orthodox churches, and I gradually began to make peace with Jesus. I also realized that most people on earth have one spiritual master who serves as their personal teacher. Through a long process that I describe in detail in *The Mystical Teachings of Jesus*, I discovered that Jesus is indeed my personal master, and this led me to the next logical step.

After I came to accept the existence of spiritual masters, it became obvious to me that they have the ability to communicate with us and that they are always willing to do so. The only limitation is our ability to hear the masters, or our willingness to consider what they have to say. Over the course of history, millions of people have experienced such communication from a higher realm, and a few people have developed the ability to serve as messengers for our spiritual masters and bring forth new teachings and ideas.

For many years I accepted this concept, yet I never considered that I might become such a messenger. Nevertheless, I came to a point where I felt I had established a personal contact with Jesus, and I realized he wanted me to bring forth new spiritual teachings. He wanted me to help him bring back the true, universal message that he presented 2,000 years ago, a message that was lost in the political shuffle of the Christian church.

The core of Jesus' message is that there is an alternative to the way of life followed by most people. We can follow a systematic path that leads us to a deeper understanding of life, a higher sense of awareness, a higher state of consciousness. We can do this by following the call of Paul to "Let this mind be in you, which was also in Christ Jesus" (Philippians 2:5). Jesus came to be an example for all of us to follow. He had no desire to be turned into an idol and worshiped as the only person who can attain a higher state of consciousness.

This book will present a universal path whereby you can achieve the state of consciousness demonstrated by Jesus and other spiritual masters. I invite you to explore this book and discover the real Jesus, the universal spiritual teacher who came to show us the way – the inner way – to true spiritual freedom!

## A practical note

The communication I have with Jesus is an intuitive communication. I have been trained by Jesus to raise my consciousness and tune in to his mind. He can then speak through me, and I either record what he says or type it directly. After training me, Jesus directed me to start a website, *www.askrealjesus.com*, on which people can ask questions that Jesus answers through me. The questions and answers are now on another website, *www. ascendedmasteranswers.com*. In many cases, my communication with Jesus begins with a question. That is why much of this book is a dialogue in which I ask a question and get the answer from Jesus. However, Jesus also gives discourses on specific topics.

This book is part of a series of books that present some of the messages I have received from Jesus. The first book in the series is *The Mystical Teachings of Jesus* and others will follow. This book was originally published with the title *Save Yourself*. This book contains about 75% of the material from that book whereas the rest plus additional material is in the next book in the series, *Climbing Higher on the Mystical Path*.

The purpose of the books is to present the universal path that Jesus attempted to teach 2,000 years ago and that he is still seeking to teach today. When you begin to follow this path, you will discover that life has a general purpose and that your life has a specific purpose. Allow Jesus to help you discover your personal mission so that you can be here below all that you are Above.

# 1 | THE SECRET OF LIFE

**Kim: Jesus, what type of people are you hoping to reach with this book?**

**Jesus:** My goal is to reach people who are open to the possibility that there is a better way to live, those who are willing to make an effort to improve their lives. My purpose for this book is to offer people a practical and systematic approach that will empower them to improve their lives.

When I walked the earth 2,000 years ago, I clearly stated my purpose for coming. I said: "I am come that they might have life, and that they might have it more abundantly" (John 10:10). That purpose has never changed.

Today, I am a spiritual being, and I am still here to offer everyone the path to the abundant life. What has changed over the past 2,000 years is that humankind has attained a much deeper understanding of many aspects of life. I have far better options for describing the way to the abundant life, and that is precisely why I am offering this book as a gift from my heart. I desire to give a very clear and concise description of the systematic path that can lead anyone to the abundant life—if they are willing to make an effort. I desire to show people that life does not have to be dominated by suffering and human limitations. It is possible for anyone to rise above the human condition and attain a more spiritually abundant life while they are still on earth. By doing so, you will also attain the goal of eternal life, meaning your permanent ascension to the spiritual realm after you leave the body and the material world.

### You are not trying to reach only Christians?

That is correct. I am seeking to reach anyone who is ready to follow a systematic path to a better life. The deciding factor is not your religious affiliation, your race, nationality, sex, age, social status or any of the other labels that people like to attach to each other. These are all outer factors.

What I am looking for is an inner quality, a condition in the core of your being. I am looking for people who are ready for the universal spiritual path that I am offering today—the same path that I came to demonstrate 2,000 years ago.

### That might surprise many people, because in my experience very few people see you as a universal teacher.

I realize that many people – Christians and non-Christians alike – have been brought up to see me as the founder of a particular religion, and many of them think I am concerned only with Christians. This is a complete fallacy because I love every lifestream, and I desire to offer every person on earth the path to a better life. I realize that many people will reject me and reject this book because they have been given a false image of me. Yet I am hoping to reach the millions of people who are ready – although some are not yet consciously aware that they are ready – to look beyond the orthodox, mainstream image of Jesus Christ and discover the true Being that I am.

The basic fact about me, and you can see this if you care to study my life, is that I never fit into people's mental boxes. For example, I did not live up to the expectations that many Jews had for the Messiah. Only few people understand that this was an essential part of my mission. The mission of the Living Christ is to teach and demonstrate that there is more to life, that there is a better way to live than the way of life experienced by most people.

How can I teach that message? How can I teach you that there is a better way to live by living my life the same way you do? How can I teach you something new if everything I say follows your expectations? I can teach you only by living a life that goes beyond your expectations so that I can hopefully shatter your mental images of what you believe is allowed or possible. I came to demonstrate that all human beings have the potential to rise above human limitations and attain the abundant life on earth and the eternal life in a higher realm.

When I say everyone, I truly mean everyone—Christian and non-Christian. In order to permanently ascend to the spiritual realm, you have to leave behind all human limitations. You leave behind the state of consciousness that causes people to feel that their religion is the only true religion and that all non-believers will go to hell. You attain a state of consciousness that is beyond all human conditionality and value judgments, a state of consciousness that is truly universal.

I am a member of a group of spiritual beings who serve as the spiritual teachers of humankind. Throughout the ages, we have been known by various names, but the name I prefer to use at this time is the "ascended masters." Our assignment from God is to help all lifestreams on earth rise above human limitations. Many of us used to be in embodiment on earth so we know the challenges faced by our unascended brothers and sisters. Because we have conquered those challenges, we are uniquely qualified to teach people how to rise above the human condition.

For millennia, the ascended masters have been working with humankind, seeking to raise people's state of consciousness and their understanding of who they are and why they are – still – on earth. As part of these efforts, we have given numerous teachings about the spiritual side of life and how to raise your consciousness. Some of these teachings were later turned into dogmatic religions, and a few of them eventually became dominated by the belief that one religion is the only true religion and the only road to salvation.

This is a fallacy. As I explain in *The Mystical Teachings of Jesus*, there is more than one true religion. The real definition of a true religion is a religion that empowers its members to rise above human limitations and attain a higher state of consciousness. That state of consciousness is universal, and to attain it, people must follow a path that is guided by certain universal laws.

One of the great achievements of science is the discovery of a set of universal laws, often called the laws of nature. Gravity is the perfect example. Gravity has the same effect on your body regardless of your religion, race, nationality or any other outer conditions. The Bible says that God is no respecter of persons (Acts 10:34), and neither is the law of gravity. Likewise, there is a set of universal laws that guide the spiritual growth of human beings. These laws do not favor people based on any outer conditions, such as membership of a particular religion or status in society. The deciding factor is a person's willingness to change, its willingness to leave behind all human beliefs and limitations. In ages past, we of the ascended masters have used a variety of spiritual teachings to help people make use of these laws. As I said, many of our efforts were turned into religions that lost their universality and became rigid and dogmatic. That is why I have decided to take a different approach in this book. I will describe the universal laws in a context that is not tied to any particular religion. I am doing this because I know that millions of people are ready to embrace a universal approach to personal and spiritual growth. These are the people I am hoping to reach with this book.

### Can you give a concise description of this universal path. I mean, what is the essence of the spiritual path that you are talking about?

In reality, you are who you are. In the here and now, you are who you think you are. There is currently a gap between who you think you are and who you really are. The essence of life, the essence of the spiritual path, is to close that gap.

### That's a pretty baffling statement!

You asked for a concise description. Ask, and you shall receive. I will be happy to give you a more detailed description.

Science has told you that everything is made from energy. Science describes energy as vibration. You know that your eyes can detect only certain types of energy, certain types of vibration, namely what you call visible light. There are many types of vibration that your eyes cannot detect, nevertheless these energies are still real. The material universe is made from energy that vibrates within a certain frequency spectrum. There are many types of energy that vibrate at frequencies outside of that spectrum. These forms of energy are invisible to the human senses and to most scientific instruments. That is why so many people, including many scientists, believe there is nothing outside the material universe.

Science has already discovered certain types of energy that vibrate at higher frequencies than those in the material universe. However, most scientists have not yet recognized these discoveries for what they are, and the results have not been interpreted correctly. These findings demonstrate that there is an entire world above and beyond the material universe. Spiritual and religious people have traditionally referred to it as Heaven, the spirit world or higher realms.

God and God's representatives have created a large number of spiritual beings. Some of these beings made the choice to descend to the material universe, including planet earth. Some of these spiritual beings lived on earth until they had fulfilled their desire to be here and then ascended back to higher realms. Other beings gradually lost connection to the spiritual realm. They lost their ability to perceive the spiritual realm, and they began to believe that the material universe is all there is. Through this process of descending into a lower state of consciousness, these beings forgot their spiritual origin. They began to see themselves as human beings.

When you were created as a spiritual being, God gave you free will. You have the ability to create an inner perception that is different from, out of touch with, the reality created by God. You can create your own world view or sense of identity, and thereby you can create the illusion that you – and the entire material universe – are separated from God. You might even believe that God does not exist. God allows you to create this illusion, however the illusion exists only inside your mind. It will continue to exist only as long as you choose to maintain it.

All of the problems manifesting on planet earth spring from the fact that human beings have forgotten their true identity as spiritual beings. They have descended into a lower state of consciousness and they have created the misery and suffering found on this planet. The only way to remove these conditions is that human beings must decide to stop creating and maintaining such conditions. People must overcome the illusion that they are limited, mortal human beings and accept the reality that they are spiritual beings.

The essence of the spiritual path is that a human being can rise above the state of consciousness that causes people to create misery and suffering. My mission on earth was meant to teach and demonstrate this fact. I came to show people a systematic path that leads them from their current state of consciousness to a higher state of consciousness. This is the essential message taught by every true religion and spiritual philosophy.

There really is only one message that we, who are the spiritual teachers of humankind, are trying to get across to those of our brothers and sisters who currently see themselves as human beings. The message is that no matter who you are right now, no matter what mistakes you might have made in the past, no matter what outer circumstances you currently experience and no matter what you believe about life, it is possible for you to rise above it all and win back a full conscious recognition of your true spiritual identity.

The essence of life is that there is a path to a higher state of consciousness in which there is no difference between who you are and who you think you are.

**It has been my experience that many people are not ready to accept the reality that we have created our own problems and that we must uncreate them. What exactly will it take for a person to be ready to accept the spiritual path?**

Before he or she is able to begin earnestly walking the spiritual
path, a person has to reach the following conclusions:

• **Change is possible.** The person must believe it is
possible to improve its life. It might reach this conclusion by observing other people overcome difficulties, by
reading books or by receiving inspiration from a spiritual
teacher, such as myself. The person might also gain an
deeper understanding of life whereby it becomes obvious why change is possible.

• **Knowledge is power.** The key to any progress seen
by humankind has been an increased understanding of
some aspect of life. If you are to improve your life, you
must begin by increasing your understanding of life. You
must make an effort to study the spiritual path and find
out how to achieve personal growth.

• **Change yourself.** Once you get understanding, you
must be willing to apply that understanding and make a
sincere effort. You must realize that the key to changing
your outer situation is to begin by changing your inner
 situation. The key to changing the world is to change
yourself.

• **Persistence is the key to progress.** In this age of
instant gratification, people must realize that personal
growth is not a mechanical process that happens instantly.
Yet if you take the right approach, you will see results. It
might not happen overnight, but it will happen.

**In my observation, one of the main obstacles to people accepting the spiritual path is that many people have come to believe that they are stuck in circumstances beyond their control. They believe there is nothing they can do to improve their lives so why bother trying? What would you say to such people?**

I would first say that if you take a look at the sketchy glimpse of my life recorded in the scriptures, I think it should be obvious that I had great compassion for people who were suffering. In reality, my entire mission was directed at helping people overcome the sense of being stuck in human limitations. I do feel great compassion for the many people who are experiencing very difficult situations and who naturally feel stuck in circumstances beyond their immediate control. I am not here trying to say that anyone can easily change any condition they face. It is possible for you to improve your life and your life experience.

I fully understand why so many people feel stuck in human limitations and feel like they could do nothing to change their circumstances. Yet I am also a spiritual teacher, and therefore I clearly see the reason people feel stuck, and the reason is a lack of understanding. The simple fact is that people feel stuck because they have not been given a proper understanding of the basic fact of life. Neither orthodox Christianity nor any other religion or philosophy – including scientific materialism – can currently give people an understanding of the secret of life. Yet once you understand that secret, you will see that you are never actually stuck. There is always something you can do to improve your situation.

**That certainly sounds intriguing. What exactly is the secret of life?**

To explain the secret of life, I would like to begin by asking you to get a mirror.

**A mirror?**

Yes, please get a mirror.

**Okay, I've got the mirror.**

Hold it up in front of you and look at the image that appears in the mirror. Let us now imagine that you want the image in the mirror to smile. How could that possibly happen?

**Well, in order to get the mirror image to smile, I would have to smile myself. Obviously, the image is just a reflection of myself so it can't change unless I change my expression.**

That is correct. Now imagine that you have a person who wants to see his mirror image smile. Yet he is simply sitting in front of the mirror with a straight face, waiting for the image in the mirror to smile. His attitude is that when the image in the mirror smiles at him, he will smile back at the image. What would you think of such a person?

**Obviously, I would think the person was ignorant about the basic facts of life. I mean, everyone knows that the mirror can only reflect back to you what you do. What has that got to do with the secret of life?**

It illustrates the secret of life. The simple fact is that God has created a universe that acts like a mirror. You are living in the center of your personal house of mirrors. You are literally the center of your own personal universe, and it will reflect back to you whatever you send out.

If you want the universe to smile at you, you must first smile at the universe. Unfortunately, most people take the same approach to life as the imaginary man takes to the mirror. They are sitting in the center of their personal house of mirrors, and they are waiting for the universe to smile at them. They have adopted the attitude that they either will not or cannot smile at the universe until the universe smiles at them.

They have allowed themselves to become trapped in a state of consciousness in which they believe they have no control over their own situation and their own destiny. They believe their happiness and well-being depends on external factors over which they have little or no control. They believe the universe is too big and powerful to be affected by their thoughts, their world view, their attitude and their state of consciousness.

In reality, the universe is made from God's energy. Energy is a passive substance that can take on any form. Yet energy cannot take on form by itself. To take on form, energy must be acted upon by the active force of a self-conscious mind. If you wait for the universe to smile at you before you are willing to smile at the universe, you have completely misunderstood the most basic fact about life in this world.

The basic fact is that human beings have the capacity of consciousness to affect God's energy. Because of that capability, you are the author and finisher of your own destiny. You create your own situation; you make your own bed and you will inevitably have to lie in it. The simple fact is that most people aren't happy about their lives, and they think they are unhappy because their outer conditions do not live up to their expectations about life. They reason that they cannot be happy until the outer situation changes. They think that if only certain conditions were different, they would automatically be happy. Yet because of what I have just explained, this is taking a backward approach.

If you want your outer situation to change, you must begin by changing your inner situation because the universe can reflect back to you only what you send out. If you want the universal mirror to show you a smiling face, you must first smile at the universe.

**I understand what you are saying, but I also think it is a very radical message that most people will find it quite difficult to accept. For one thing, where is the connection between what you just said and the teachings you gave us 2,000 years ago?**

The connection is very direct. I said essentially the same thing 2,000 years ago, I simply used different words. The reason was that in those days people did not have the understanding that most people have today. They did not understand energy so I could not give them a more profound teaching. That is why I spoke to the multitudes in parables and taught all things to my disciples (Mark 4:34). Yet even my disciples could not understand the concept that everything is made from energy.

If you read the scriptures, you will see that the message I just gave you is woven through my teachings. The most obvious example is the concept of turning the other cheek (Matthew 5:39), of doing unto others what you would have them do unto you (Luke 6:31). Don't you see the clear connection to the fact that the universe is a mirror which reflects back to you what you send out?

I am well-aware that because of the distortion created by orthodox Christianity, most people have misunderstood this concept. Because of the consciousness of guilt and fear that took over the Christian religion, most people look upon my commandments as dictates that carry the threat of eternal damnation and punishment. They think I was telling them to turn the other cheek because if they don't, they will burn forever in hell. Yet what I am talking about here is simply enlightened self-interest. Hell is something people create with their own consciousness. Because their outer situation is a reflection of their inner situation, they will be trapped in imperfect circumstances, some of which rightfully deserve to be called hell on earth, until they change their state of mind. Paul understood this, and that is why he told people to: "Let this mind be in you, which was also in Christ Jesus" (Philippians 2:5).

Imagine that you walk down the street and suddenly see a man who runs headfirst into a concrete wall. He almost knocks himself out, but he manages to get back on his feet, and he runs right into the wall again. Obviously, you would think that the person was odd. When he gets a concussion, you would never think to blame the concrete wall for his injuries. It would be obvious to you that the man brought his misfortune upon himself. After all, anyone should have known that if you pound your head against a concrete wall, you end up hurting yourself.

In reality, most people are pounding their heads against the concrete wall of the universe, and then they turn around and blame the universe, God or other people for the fact that they get a headache. Some even spend the rest of their lives trying to change the universe instead of changing themselves so that the cosmic mirror can reflect back a better image.

Most people think that my message to do unto others as you would have them do unto you is a fear-based message.

They think that if they don't follow my "dictate," they will be punished by God by burning forever in hell. In truth, my message was not fear-based but reality-based. I was simply trying to tell people that if they pound their heads against a concrete wall, they will hurt themselves. If they frown at the universe, the universe will frown back at them. I wasn't warning people about what will happen to them after death. I was trying to tell them how to improve life here on earth. I was trying to tell them that they will be trapped in limitations and suffering until they change their approach to life, their state of consciousness.

If you treat other people the way you want to be treated, the entire universe will treat you the way you have treated others. The simple reason is that the universe will inevitably reflect back to you what you send out. It is up to you to take the first step because the universal mirror can only reflect your own actions back to you. Don't you see the obvious connection to my old teachings?

**Yes, I do see it, and I am quite frankly embarrassed that I never realized that truth before. It is very obvious to me the way you explain it.**

Well, there is no need to be embarrassed. You didn't know, and when you don't know better, you simply cannot do better. That is why the key to improving your life is to expand your understanding of life. I am quite aware that this idea has many profound and subtle ramifications, and for most people it will take some time and effort to fully absorb and integrate this message. I know it will take time for people to change their lives according to this truth. That is why I told people that in their patience they shall possess their souls (Luke 21:19).

Nevertheless, I caution people against becoming overly patient with themselves.

As I said, your outer situation simply cannot change until you begin to change your inner situation. By delaying the change of consciousness, you are only delaying the day when you will see improvement in your outer situation. Truly, God does not punish human beings. Human beings punish themselves because they create their outer situation according to their state of consciousness.

## 2 | LEAVING THE SCHOOL OF HARD KNOCKS

**Let me pick up on your statement that if people knew better, they would do better. What exactly do you mean by that—I know lots of people who seem to know better, yet they are not doing better. What about the many people who knowingly hurt others?**

My statement is true, but you might have to add that there is knowledge and there is understanding. I agree that many people have an outer, intellectual knowledge that certain acts are wrong, yet they still carry out such acts. The reason is that they have not attained a true, inner understanding, they have not fully internalized the fact that they simply cannot escape the consequences of their actions.

If such people fully understood that the universe is a mirror, they would realize – with absolute certainty – that when they harm another person, the universe will reflect those actions back to them at some point in the future. They would know that the Bible is absolutely correct when it states: "Be not deceived; God is not mocked: for whatsoever a man soweth, that shall he also reap" (Galatians 6:7). This statement is simply a dramatic way of saying that the universe is a mirror.

I realize that people do some strange things, but it is a fact that most of the people who violate the rights of others do so because they are very self-centered and selfish. If these people truly understood that their actions were hurting themselves, they would not commit those acts. No human being will knowingly hurt him- or herself, and the most selfish people are the least likely to hurt themselves. Once again, the problem is ignorance.

**In my observation, many people don't want to know better. They don't want to know about the consequences of their actions, and they don't want to acknowledge that they can do something to improve their lives. This has always amazed me, and I am wondering if you agree with my observation?**

Of course. The unwillingness to expand your understanding of life is the major problem I run into as a spiritual teacher. Many people have closed their minds and hearts so firmly that I have no chance of reaching them with a true spiritual teaching.

Unfortunately, many of the people with the most tightly closed minds are sitting in their Christian churches every Sunday, thinking that because they belong to the only true religion, they will automatically be saved. They have overlooked the fact that I systematically challenged the scribes, the Pharisees, the Sadducees, the lawyers and anyone else who had used outer doctrines as an excuse for closing their minds to my teachings. Obviously, you find closed-minded and open-minded people in every walk of life.

**What could possibly help such people open their
minds to the spiritual path? I mean, finding the spiritual path made a tremendous difference in my life.
Since then I have felt a desire to help other people
experience the same joy and peace in their lives so
I have often been contemplating how to help people discover and accept the spiritual path. I have
been struggling to understand why some people
have closed their minds so I would be grateful if you
could give me a deeper understanding of why so
many ignore or reject the path?**

I share your hope that all people on earth can eventually discover and follow the true spiritual path. Yet I have worked
with lifestreams for these past 2,000 years, seeking to inspire
them to discover that path. During this work, I have encountered every conceivable explanation or excuse that people have
for not embracing the spiritual path or improving their lives.
I must tell you that it currently is not possible to inspire every
human being on earth to accept the spiritual path. The reason
being that before a lifestream can accept the spiritual path, it
must have reached a certain level of inner maturity. Let me
explain that in more detail.

When you, as a human being, approach a person and tell
him or her about the spiritual path, you will encounter the
outer reason that the soul gives for ignoring or rejecting the
path. However, such outer reasons are not the real reasons for
rejecting the path. As a spiritual teacher, I have the ability to
see through the outer reasons, to look deep within the psyche
of the lifestream and discover the subconscious causes. I can
tell you that there is basically only one reason why lifestreams
ignore or reject the path.

Before I tell you the reason, I would like to say that there is one message I would like to get across to all human beings. That message is the fact that the spiritual teachers of humankind do not judge people according to a human standard. We do not set up an outer standard for how a person should be, and we do not impose value judgments upon people. We have transcended all human judgment. We feel only unconditional love for every human being on earth. Yet the love that we feel is also beyond human love, which is always conditional. Most people use an outer standard to judge whether someone is worthy to receive their love. We have no such standard and we impose no such judgment. We give our love freely to all; our love truly rains upon the just and the unjust (Matthew 5:45), but our love is not blind.

Unconditional love sees everything that takes place in the lifestream without placing a value judgment upon what it sees. What I am about to say is not meant to be construed as a judgment of people. I am not condemning any person, I am simply stating my observation as a spiritual teacher who has observed billions of lifestreams respond – or not respond – to the spiritual path. Over the past 2,000 years, I have approached every lifestream on earth at inner levels – although most people are not consciously aware of this – and offered them the path to a more abundant life.

My observation is that when it comes to accepting the spiritual path, the deciding factor is whether the lifestream has come to the point of being willing to take responsibility for itself, for its life and for its salvation. If a lifestream has not reached the point of inner maturity that empowers it to take responsibility for itself, the lifestream simply cannot accept the spiritual path. It will either ignore that path, explain it away as unimportant or deny it altogether.

When the lifestream has not yet reached the critical state of maturity, it simply cannot accept the basic fact of life, namely that human beings will reap what they have sown, and therefore it is up to each person to improve its life and secure its salvation. The person simply cannot accept that it needs to change itself in order to improve its situation and be saved.

When the lifestream is not ready to take responsibility for itself, it must find a way to avoid feeling responsible for its situation, for its spiritual progress and for its salvation. The spiritual path is a process whereby a lifestream can take active measures to raise its state of consciousness, until it finally escapes the limitations found on earth and permanently ascends to the spiritual realm. If the lifestream cannot accept responsibility, it must find a way to ignore or reject the spiritual path. There is an almost infinite variety of such explanations, but they can be put into the following categories:

  • **Ignorance.** Some lifestreams accept a belief system that portrays them as victims of circumstances beyond their control. The person can do nothing to save itself but must passively wait for a savior outside itself. Incidentally, the doctrines presented by some Christian churches spring from and encourage this belief. Such churches claim that human beings are sinners by nature and can be saved only through the grace of God administered by myself.

  • **Fear.** Another common reaction is that you shouldn't or that you are not allowed to do anything to save yourself. One example of this is scientific materialism, which claims that there is no God and therefore walking the spiritual path is just superstition. Another example is the orthodox belief that it is blasphemy to think you can follow in my footsteps

• **Indifference.** Some people are so caught up in their material lives that they have no attention left over for the spiritual side of life. They simply don't think they have to do anything to save themselves, and they are completely indifferent to the spiritual path.

Billions of people on this earth are currently trapped in one of these approaches to life. Yet we have entered a new spiritual age in which millions of lifestreams are rapidly approaching the point of maturity that empowers them to take responsibility for themselves and for their spiritual path. This is my main motivation for bringing out this book. I am hoping to reach out to these people and demonstrate that there is indeed a universal spiritual path. This path transcends not only all religions but also the philosophy of scientific materialism that has affected so many people in today's world.

I am clearly aware that many of the lifestreams who have reached the critical level of inner maturity have also attained the ability to see through some of the hypocrisy of orthodox religion. Many of them have rejected all religion, including Christianity. While I understand this reaction, I have to say it is not a constructive reaction because it will not give people peace of mind. The mature lifestream knows, at subconscious levels, that there is a spiritual side to life. If the person's conscious mind rejects the spiritual reality, there will be a tension, a conflict, in the soul.

What you see in today's world is that many mature lifestreams feel this inner tension, but because they do not understand the cause, they are seeking to cover it up instead of resolving it. There are three main reactions by people who are trying to cover over the inner conflict in their lifestreams:

• Some people adopt the philosophy of scientific materialism – or a similar philosophy – and deny the validity of anything spiritual. They often use the perceived hypocrisy and shortcomings of orthodox religion as a justification for doing this.

• Some people become very fervent in their religious beliefs. That is indeed why you see so many people who cling to traditional beliefs and are not willing to consider anything that questions those doctrines. These people can often become almost fanatical in defending their religious beliefs, and they refuse to look at anything beyond orthodox doctrines. You especially see this in Christianity and Islam.

• Some people simply want to run away from the inner pain in their souls. They might seek to escape by focusing all of their attention on achieving some outer goal, such as a career, a family, power, money, sex or other material pleasures or possessions. They might even seek temporary escape through drugs, alcohol or other addictions.

The common thread behind all of these reactions is that in today's age many lifestreams are maturing spiritually, and they realize there is more to life. Because they grew up in a culture that denies the existence of true spirituality, they do not know where to look for that something. They cannot resolve the tension in their souls. It is my hope that this book can reach some of these people and help them understand why they cannot be satisfied by anything they are doing. I hope to help them see that this is not because there is something wrong with them. It is caused by the fact that their lifestreams have reached a level of maturity where they are ready to discover and walk the spiritual path. Only by following that path can they remove the inner tension and begin to feel at peace with themselves. Over these past decades, millions of people have followed the spiritual path in one form or another. Yet millions more of ready for that path and have not yet discovered it. I hope this book can help some of these people.

**Is there nothing that can be done to help a lifestream discover the path until that person reaches the critical level of maturity?**

You cannot help a lifestream discover the spiritual path until it is ready to take responsibility for itself. It would be like seeking to teach a newborn baby to walk before its body has developed the strength to stand up. The lifestream must come to the point of being willing to change itself and take active measures to improve its lot in life. As long as the lifestream is taking a passive approach to life, waiting for something or someone outside itself to solve its problems, you cannot help that lifestream accept the spiritual path because the path is a do-it-yourself process.

**You earlier said that many lifestreams are ready to discover the spiritual path, but some of them are not consciously aware of this fact. I assume that many of these people feel the inner longing you are talking about, yet their outer minds cannot accept the spiritual path. Is that correct.**

Yes, that is quite true.

### Isn't there some idea that might help these people get over the hump and consciously realize that they are longing to find the spiritual path?

It can be helpful for some lifestreams to consider the idea that planet earth is a cosmic schoolroom. Your lifestream descended to earth partly because it wanted to learn how to use God's energy. One might say that this planet is a kind of science lab that teaches lifestreams how to use energy. The important point in this context is that there are two ways to learn in the schoolroom of earth. One is the conscious way of learning and the other is the unconscious way. One is the spiritual path, and the other is the School of Hard Knocks.

Let us reach back to my statement that there is a set of universal laws that guide the spiritual growth of lifestreams. The most important of these laws is the Law of Free Will. God has given you free will to experiment with his energy. You can use this energy to create whatever you want, and the only catch is that whatever you create will be reflected back to you by the cosmic mirror. You will inevitably experience the conditions you create. I will later explain when and how people created the conditions they currently face.

When a lifestream begins to take responsibility for itself, it becomes possible for the lifestream to recognize that God has not created the limitations and suffering you currently see on earth. God's original design for this planet did not include human suffering and pain. God wanted people to learn by experiencing only positive consequences of their actions. Yet because God gave lifestreams free will, God could not prevent them from using their free will to create unpleasant consequences.

Most of the world's religions teach the concept that, in a past era, life was without suffering. Yet because of a particular event, human beings have descended from that pure estate. In the Bible, you find the concept of the Garden of Eden and the Fall of Man. This story is not meant to be taken literally. It is a metaphor that is meant to illustrate the fact that in the distant past – so distant that neither orthodox Christians nor scientists would accept the true time frame – lifestreams lived in a protected environment. We might consider the Garden of Eden as a school that was set up to give lifestreams a safe framework for learning how to use energy. The "God" in the Garden was not God in the ultimate sense. It was a member of the ascended masters who served as the spiritual teacher for a group of lifestreams. This teacher, whose name is Maitreya, offered lifestreams a path of conscious learning. The teacher had attained a high degree of mastery, and his students had a chance to learn from his experience and insights.

In this mystery school, the students consciously knew that they were spiritual beings. They knew their lifestreams were created in a higher realm and had voluntarily descended into the denser vibrations of the material universe. They also knew that a part of themselves, what we might call the spiritual self or I AM Presence, permanently resides in the spiritual realm. They experienced a conscious connection to their spiritual selves.

At some point, a group of students became impatient with the graded lessons offered by the teacher. They were tempted into taking one of the advanced lessons before they were ready for it. That lesson was to experiment with what the Bible calls the "tree of the knowledge of good and evil." In reality, this is a symbol for a state of consciousness that is based on duality. You see, in the Garden lifestreams had a sense of oneness with their spiritual selves and with the teacher. Yet when they partook of the consciousness of duality, they lost that sense of oneness. As a result, they lost their sense of identity as spiritual beings and they lost contact with the teacher.

In reality, lifestreams were not forcefully cast out of the garden. They gradually lowered the vibrations of their consciousness until they lost contact with their spiritual teacher and lost all memory of their spiritual origin. This was never God's original desire or plan, but because God had given lifestreams free will, he could not stop their descent without violating his own law. Yet when God gave lifestreams free will, he knew that some of them might misuse his energy to create a sense of identity as being separated from their source. If that happened, such lifestreams could no longer learn by following a spiritual teacher and the spiritual path. God had to provide another way for lifestreams to learn, and he did so by designing the material universe as a mirror.

When lifestreams lost their contact with the spiritual teacher, the cosmic mirror became their teacher. Unfortunately, because people had lost contact with their teacher, there was no way to tell them about this. They had descended from the path of conscious learning to the path of unconscious learning—the School of Hard Knocks. In this school you learn by seeing the consequences of your actions as they are mirrored back to you by the universe.

Instead of being taught by a loving teacher, who has walked the path and knows the bumps in the road, you must now learn by experiencing the consequences of your actions. Obviously, this can be a very difficult learning process, and it can take a long time to realize what is going on. That is why the ascended masters have attempted to send humankind spiritual teachers who could teach them how the universe works. It has been our hope to bring people back into the cosmic mystery school, the school of conscious learning. We have sought to accomplish this goal by giving people a variety of spiritual teachings that originally taught elements of the universal spiritual path.

It is very difficult to reach lifestreams who are in the school of unconscious learning. One reason is that because the universe is a mirror, people's beliefs and attitudes tend to become self-fulfilled prophecies. If you believe God is an angry and judgmental God who is ready to punish you for the slightest mistake, you will send a lot of fear-based energy into the universe. When that energy is reflected back to you by the cosmic mirror, you tend to see it as God's punishment, and this will reinforce your negative image of God. It is quite difficult to help souls see beyond the false image of an angry God and help them realize that God is a God of unconditional love.

**That is a fascinating thought, because it explains why people can become so stuck in certain beliefs. They think life is a certain way because God or evolution created it that way, and they cannot see that they actually created their own misery. What could possibly break this spell?**

There is a higher and a lower, a conscious and an unconscious, way to break the spell. Let us first look at how some people overcome the spell through the School of Hard Knocks.

When a lifestream descends into the material universe, it becomes subject to the laws that God used to create the material world. Because everything in the material world is made from energy, one of the most fundamental laws is the Law of Cause and Effect. In the material universe, everything the lifestream does, including thoughts, feelings and actions, is done with God's energy. The Law of Cause and Effect states that a lifestream is ultimately responsible for how it uses God's energy.

What keeps you alive in the material world is a constant stream of high-frequency energy from your spiritual self. This energy flows into the your lower vehicle, what many people call the soul, and you express it through your subconscious and conscious minds. In the process of expressing this energy, you change its vibration. You can compare this to shining a beam of white light into a glass prism. The prism splits the light into the colors of the rainbow. Likewise, your subconscious and conscious minds split the pure light from your spiritual self into various colors, or vibrations.

We can also use the analogy of a film projector. The light coming from your spiritual self is like the white light that shines from the bulb in the projector. Your subconscious and conscious minds are like filmstrips. The images you hold in your mind will color the white light from the spiritual self. When the light passes through the filmstrip, it takes on the colors and images that are on the strip. What is projected on the screen of life – the cosmic mirror – is simply an image of what is in your conscious and subconscious minds.

If you use energy in harmony with the laws of God, you will change the vibration of spiritual energy, but it will never go below a certain frequency. When you look at energy frequencies, you will discover a dividing line, a threshold. Above the dividing line, you find only beneficial, or constructive, energy. Such vibrations will serve to expand and enhance God's creation and your creative abilities. This is illustrated in my parable about the servants who multiplied their talents (Matthew 25:14-30). When you have been faithful over a few things, God will make you ruler over a greater amount of creative energy. Any energy below the critical frequency will serve to break down and limit creation, including your own creative powers. When you misuse energy, you create negative consequences for yourself, and you will inevitably experience it as pain and suffering.

We might say that when lifestreams first descended to earth, God provided them with a staircase that could lead them toward greater and greater freedom and creative expression. Instead of ascending the staircase, some lifestreams started descending it. As they did, they descended into a basement that eventually became smaller and smaller. The consequences you create by misusing God's energy will create a box around your soul. As you continue to create limiting consequences, the box becomes smaller and smaller until you can no longer move.

Some lifestreams finally feel so boxed in by pain and suffering that they cry out: "I can't do this anymore. There must be a better way; there must be more to life!" The lifestream finally decides that it no longer wants to descend the staircase and that it wants to escape suffering and pain. One of the laws that guide the growth of lifestreams is expressed in the saying: "When the student is ready, the teacher appears." At the moment a lifestream sincerely reaches for a better way, it will find some thought or philosophy that can serve as a lifeline. This might be an outer religion that offers the lifestream some guidelines for how to improve its life.

Unfortunately, many of the lifestreams who descend far down the staircase are not ready for the true spiritual path. They are so burdened by their self-created consequences that they are not ready to accept responsibility for themselves. Consequently, such souls look for a religion that promises salvation through an outer savior. These lifestreams simply want to escape the unpleasant circumstances they experience, yet they are not ready to admit that they have created those conditions. They are not willing to change themselves in order to change what is mirrored back to them by the universe. It can take such lifestreams a long time to reach the point of maturity that empowers them to find the spiritual path and begin the process of conscious learning. Yet a lifestream can, at any time, decide to awaken itself and join the path of consciously improving its life.

It is helpful for people to ponder the image that life on earth can be compared to a staircase. You can ascend the staircase or you can descend it. If you descend the staircase, you automatically enroll yourself in the School of Hard Knocks. If you keep going in that direction, the knocks will become harder and harder until you decide that you have had enough. The reason is that it is your own misuse of energy that creates the knocks.

This can be understood by considering the scientific discovery of the law of action and reaction. For every action, there is an opposite reaction of equal intensity. If you allow yourself to descend into a very self-centered state of consciousness, you will send a very intense action of toxic energy into the universe. It is inevitable that the universe will respond with an opposite reaction of equal intensity. The scientific law of action and reaction should have allowed people to abandon the ancient concept that God is punishing their sins.

God does not punish people at all. Your lifestream made the choice to turn your back upon the spiritual teacher, and thereby you enrolled yourself in the School of Hard Knocks. God has simply designed the universe as a mirror so by sending out toxic energy, you will inevitably punish yourself. God has no desire to see you continue punishing yourself. We who are your spiritual teachers have no desire to see you continue to punish yourself. We are always ready to offer you the spiritual path, but we cannot do so until you accept responsibility for yourself and realize that if your outer situation is to change, you must first change yourself. You are the only one who can decide to reverse course, and to do that many lifestreams unfortunately have to reach a breaking point. They have to "hit rock bottom," as is the case for many addicts.

As a spiritual teacher, I love nothing more than to see a lifestream turn around before it reaches the breaking point. This does indeed happen to some lifestreams, and it happens when they start using the reasoning faculties of the mind.

**I share that hope. What can help a person turn around before it hits rock bottom?**

Obviously, this is individual to every lifestream so it is difficult to formulate one particular philosophy that will work equally well for everyone. Nevertheless, one of the most helpful ideas is the fact that lifestreams descended to earth because they have a desire to experience the material world. Yet the desire for experiences springs from a deeper desire, which is the desire to learn how God's creation works so that the lifestream can become a co-creator with God and help create a better world.

There are two ways to learn how creation works. One is through direct observation and experience, and the other is through the reasoning faculties of the mind. As as simple example, think back to my earlier story of a man who runs headfirst into a concrete wall. Imagine that you have a lifestream who is new on earth so it does not know much about life on this planet. You might tell such a person that if he runs headfirst into a concrete wall, he will hurt himself, but the lifestream really has no bank of experiences that allows it to relate to what you are saying.

It might be necessary for the lifestream to run into the concrete wall in order to truly experience what happens. Yet after the lifestream has had the experience that running into a hard object causes pain, it should be able to transfer this experience to other situations. If you take the lifestream to a wall that is built from stones instead of concrete, the lifestream should be able to reason that since the stones feel about as hard as concrete, running into the stone wall would cause pain. The lifestream really should not need to experience what it feels like to run into a stone wall. It should be possible for the lifestream to use the reasoning faculties of the mind without experiencing the pain on the physical body.

Even though the lifestream has a built-in desire for experiences, it does not need to experience every possible form of human suffering in order to decide that it is willing to come up higher. You should not need to experience every aspect of human misery in order to decide that there must be a better way to live.

As I said, there are two ways to learn in the schoolroom of earth. One is through direct experience, which is the School of Hard Knocks. The other is through reasoning where you use the mind to imagine what a particular experience would feel like without actually going through the experience. Thereby, you can decide to rise above a certain situation without actually hurting yourself. This way of learning is the spiritual path.

I earlier said that you cannot make a lifestream aware of the spiritual path until it has reached a certain maturity. One might say that the lifestream must reach a turning point. The turning point is where the lifestream decides that it no longer wants to be enrolled in the School of Hard Knocks. The lifestream decides that it has experienced enough pain and suffering and that it wants a better life.

When the lifestream decides that it no longer wants to continue in the School of Hard Knocks, it is ready to meet a spiritual teacher, and the spiritual teacher will inevitably appear in whatever form the lifestream can currently accept. At that point, the lifestream can – if it takes advantage of what the teacher offers – begin to learn from the teacher instead of learning exclusively through its own experiences. I am sure you have heard the saying that there is no point in reinventing the wheel. Imagine that every lifestream on earth had to learn only through its own experiences. The consequence would be that every lifestream had to go through a certain amount of misery before it finally decided that it had experienced enough human suffering. When it made that decision, it would have to discover on its own how to rise to a higher state of consciousness. It is almost as if there were no schools that taught children how to read and write. Every child had to invent the alphabet on its own.

If this truly had been the conditions found on earth, humankind would never have risen above the stage of the cave people. The fact that we today see a much more sophisticated civilization, demonstrates that there is an alternative to learning from direct experience. Instead of learning exclusively from your own experiences, you can use the reasoning faculties of the mind to learn from the experiences of others. You do not have to make every possible human mistake. You need to have a certain amount of experiences so you realize that some conditions lead to suffering. Yet when your lifestream is saturated with such experiences, it can observe the lives of other people and reason that many other activities also lead to suffering. The lifestream can therefore decide that it does not need to go through these situations but that it is willing to learn from a teacher.

This is the basic idea behind the concept of the spiritual path. The reality of life on earth is that, throughout the ages, a few lifestreams in every generation have discovered how to rise above the human consciousness that leads to pain and suffering. They have risen above the School of Hard Knocks and have discovered the school of conscious learning. Some of these lifestreams have passed the final exam in the schoolroom of earth and have ascended to the spiritual realm. Out of love for their brothers and sisters, who are still stuck on earth, they have decided to join the ascended masters. We are the spiritual teachers who work with people on earth, seeking to inspire them to leave the School of Hard Knocks and follow the spiritual path. We do this by giving people many forms of spiritual teachings, and the original teachings behind every true religion on earth were given by the ascended masters for the purpose of helping a specific group of lifestreams rise to a higher level of consciousness.

When people get tired of learning in the School of Hard Knocks, we of the ascended masters offer them an alternative in the form of what I have called the spiritual path. Yet that path is very diversified and there truly is something that can appeal to every person on earth, no matter what state of consciousness they currently experience. If people will ask with an open mind and heart, they will surely find something that will help them rise above the School of Hard Knocks and find a better way to learn.

Yet the bottom line is that you can lead a person to water, but you cannot make him or her drink. If people insist on staying in the School of Hard Knocks, there is not much you can do. There are truly some souls who seem intent on experiencing every type of human misery and limitation. As a spiritual teacher, I can only stand by and wait for them to reach the turning point and decide that they have – finally – had enough. This book is offered to lifestreams who have already made that decision.

## 3 | THE KEY OF KNOWLEDGE

Let us say that a person has come to the turning point and is either feeling that there must be more to life or has already realized that there is a path to a better life, how would you advise such a person to start walking the path? I mean, when I first became aware of the path, it seemed quite overwhelming to me. I needed something very concrete and practical that I could grab on to and use as a lifeline to pull myself up.

When I discovered the path, I wasn't ready for a very sophisticated understanding of the spiritual side of life. I felt like a drowning person who was struggling to catch my breath. After a while, I got my head above the water, I began to look around and I gradually discovered a deeper understanding of the path. But in the beginning, I just needed something simple and practical. What is your advice on how to get started?

The image of a drowning person is a good illustration of how many people feel just before they discover the path. Some people go through a personal crisis that opens their minds to discovering the path, and they do need a very concrete, practical lifeline as their on-ramp to the spiritual path. For some people it becomes a self-help philosophy, perhaps a business-related empowerment technique. For others it might be a traditional religion or a New Age organization. For people with addictions, it might be a 12-step program or another recovery program. It really isn't that important exactly what serves as the on-ramp because whatever it is, it will be what the person needs in order to take the next step. The important point is that people don't become emotionally attached to the organization or technique that introduced them to the path and think it has all they will ever need.

It is important to keep in mind that the spiritual path is a highly individual process. Each person is unique and needs to go through a set of personalized steps in order to complete his or her path. That is why it is so dangerous when people subscribe to the belief that a particular organization is the only key to salvation and has everything a person will ever need. The spiritual path is a process with several stages. What you need in the beginning is not what you need at the end, just as a kindergarten student has different needs than a senior in college. Both are students, but they are clearly at different levels of learning.

It is true that for many people the path can seem somewhat overwhelming in the beginning, and therefore they need a lifeline to get them anchored on the path. The best way to overcome the sense of being overwhelmed is to select a teaching and a practical tool that becomes your bread and butter. You need something concrete and practical that you can use as your foundation on the path. You can later branch out from there and look for a more sophisticated teaching or a set of more efficient tools.

In order to help people overcome the sense of feeling overwhelmed, let me point out that the two key words that will help you move forward on the spiritual path are the two "Rs," namely Revelation and Ritual. The foundation for your progress is that you must increase your understanding of life— what I call receiving personal revelation about some aspect of life. The best way to accomplish that is to study a variety of spiritual teachings. Yet study in itself will not give you maximum progress because the ideas you learn must be put into practice. You need to find a practical technique that is designed to increase your spiritual growth, and you need to practice that technique faithfully—what I call ritual.

There are numerous teachings and techniques that can help people attain growth, and each person needs to find a teaching and a tool that appeals to him or her at the person's present level of spiritual maturity. I will later present some tools that can help people grow, but for now I will talk about how to get the best results from studying spiritual teachings. In order to get started on the path, it is helpful to keep in mind that when you take a walk, you use both legs. The two legs that will carry you forward on the spiritual path is to study spiritual teachings and to practice some form of ritual. These two legs are the two Rs.

**Can you tell us more about why people have different reactions and needs when they first find the path?**

Let us begin by clarifying the goal of the spiritual path. I have said that the goal is to attain a higher state of consciousness, namely what I demonstrated 2,000 years ago. I am fully aware that because Christianity became a sectarian and dogmatic religion, the term "Christ" is no longer seen as universal by most people. Yet in reality the term "Christ" is a universal name for a higher state of consciousness, and that is why I will use it in this book. The true message that I came to give people is that every human being has the potential to attain the Christ consciousness—even without becoming a member of a Christian church.

I will later describe this state of consciousness in greater detail. For now, let me say that when a lifestream first descends to earth, it has a conscious connection to its spiritual self. The lifestream knows that it is a spiritual being who originated in a higher realm. We might say that the lifestream's sense of identity is centered around the spiritual world and the I AM Presence. The lifestream is meant to gradually expand its sense of identity until it no longer sees itself as being merely connected to the I AM Presence. It comes to fully identify itself as an extension of, an individualization of, the I AM Presence. At that point the lifestream attains Christ consciousness and exclaims: "I and my Father – meaning the I AM Presence – are one!"

We might say that planet earth was designed as a schoolroom that offered lifestreams a spiral staircase that leads to Christ consciousness. When a lifestream begins to experiment with the tree of the knowledge of good and evil, it begins to descend into a consciousness of duality whereby it gradually comes to see itself as separated from the I AM Presence. As the lifestream descends the spiral staircase, it eventually forgets its spiritual origin. Consequently, its sense of identity is no longer centered on the spiritual self. Instead, the lifestream now builds a new sense of self, a pseudo self, and it begins to identify itself with this human ego. The lifestream becomes ego-centered instead of God-centered.

Although there is a lower limit beyond which a lifestream cannot descend (and remain on earth), a lifestream can go very far below the level of the Christ consciousness. Imagine that you draw a vertical line that represents people's state of consciousness, and at the top is the Christ consciousness. Most people on earth have descended below the level of the Christ consciousness, and some people have gone very far into the depths of self-centeredness. If you look at people's consciousness, you will see that some people are extremely ego-centered. They have no attention for the spiritual side of life, and they often have no concern for the rights and the suffering of other people. Some of these people are not ready for the spiritual path that I am talking about in this book. Yet no matter how low a lifestream descends, it is always possible that the lifestream can experience a turnaround.

As I said earlier, some people eventually box themselves in so tightly that they can no longer move, and they cry out for deliverance. It is a sad fact that many people begin their upward climb as the result of a severe personal crisis that finally makes them decide that they cannot keep descending the spiral staircase. I am hoping this book can help people turn around before they hit bottom.

People who are completely ego-centered have vastly different needs than people who are further up the staircase. The lower people descend, the more closed their minds become. They become very centered on the ego, and they will often reject any idea that goes beyond what the ego wants them to believe. Such people might be open only to a very simple and rigid philosophy, such as a dogmatic religion that is focused on escaping God's punishment. These people cannot grasp a deeper understanding of the spiritual side of life. It simply isn't possible for me to bring forth a book that works equally well for all people. I have to select a certain range of people as the target audience for this book, and it is my purpose to help people who have passed one of the major turning points on the spiritual path.

You might say that the spiritual path has many small steps but that it has three major stages. The lowest stage is when people have forgotten their spiritual origin and identity. They are, so to speak, lost in ignorance. These people are not yet ready to take responsibility for their spiritual growth so they need a simple and simplistic philosophy. The next phase is when lifestreams have matured to the point where they are ready to be reminded of their spiritual origin. These lifestreams can very quickly be awakened and start consciously following the path. The third stage comes when people reconnect – within themselves – to their I AM Presence and earnestly begin the phase that leads to personal Christhood.

My goal for this and the following book is to reach out to the two latter categories of people. In this book, I will present a set of practical tools for lifestreams who are ready to start the spiritual path. These tools can help a person win back a full recognition of his or her spiritual origin. For some, this awakening can happen very quickly. In the next book, I will present a set of ideas and tools for people who are ready for the final stage of putting on the mind of Christ. One might say that I am directing this book at the people who have reached a certain level of inner maturity and are now ready to consciously walk the path that will lead them all the way home.

### What is the first practical tool you want to give us?

It is a tool that I described 2,000 years ago when I rebuked the lawyers: "Woe unto you, lawyers! for ye have taken away the key of knowledge: ye entered not in yourselves, and them that were entering in ye hindered" (Luke 11:52).

In order to fully understand the "key of knowledge," let us begin by comparing the society of the cave man with modern civilization. We see a tremendous amount of progress, and the driving force behind it is that in every generation some people have dared to look beyond their present beliefs and reach for a higher understanding of a particular aspect of life.

This drive for a higher understanding, this curiosity, is actually built into the lifestream. Some lifestreams manage to beat down their curiosity until it is hardly noticeable, but it is still there as a background noise that can never be silenced completely. When a lifestream matures and is ready to embrace the spiritual path, its curiosity is usually let out of the cage, and, at least for a time, the lifestream eagerly studies new teachings and explores new horizons of the mind. Curiosity, a thirst for a higher understanding, is the rocket fuel that drives your spiritual growth. The key to making maximum progress on the spiritual path is to never allow yourself to limit or stop your curiosity.

**To me, that is a very important concept because, in the over 30 years I have been on the spiritual path, I have seen many people go through an initial awakening that suddenly makes them realize that the path exists. For a time, these people are extremely enthusiastic and eagerly study any spiritual teaching they can get their minds on. Then, after a while they either become disappointed or they join a particular organization and begin to believe it has all they need.**

**This is amazing to me because I clearly see that what gets us started on the spiritual path is that we are searching for something. It never made sense**

**to me that we suddenly think we have found it and then stop seeking. What is your take on that?**

You are quite right. The simple fact it that the driving force behind progress, from the outer progress seen by humankind to the spiritual progress of an individual, is the search for understanding. If you stop searching, it is inevitable that your progress will slow down or stop. If you are no longer making progress, you are no longer on the path to Christhood.

As a spiritual teacher, I face a very delicate challenge. My goal is to raise every lifestream from its current level of consciousness to the Christ consciousness. To do that, I must seek to give a lifestream a greater understanding, and I must keep doing so until the lifestream reaches Christ consciousness. Yet even when you reach Christ consciousness, you will not stop searching. On the contrary, you realize that creation is an ongoing process, and therefore there is always more to learn about God.

**When I first heard about the concept that we can ascend to the spiritual realm, I rejected the idea. I thought it meant we would no longer learn, and I simply couldn't conceive of not learning something new.**

I can assure you that attaining Christ consciousness does not mean that you stop learning. It means that you gain access to the mind of God, and the mind of God is infinite. I have been an ascended master for 2,000 years, and I have not explored all aspects of the mind of God.

The consequence is that as long as you are in a human body, it is safe to assume that there is always more to learn. You can never allow yourself to become emotionally attached to the teachings of a particular belief system. One of the greatest obstacles I run into as a spiritual teacher is that so many people fall into the trap of thinking that they have now found the one true religion or the ultimate philosophy—and therefore they can or should close their minds to any ideas that go beyond its doctrines.

Once you adopt this attitude, your spiritual progress comes to a crawl and, as you pointed out earlier, many people discover the path only to later crash and burn. I would very much like to see the readers of this book avoid this trap—or get out of it if they have already been there.

The key is to realize that spiritual growth is an ongoing process that can continue indefinitely, and therefore you can never stop looking for the teacher. As I said earlier, the spiritual path has a number of stages. One might compare it to a staircase between the floors in a building. When a person discovers the spiritual path, that person is on a particular floor – a particular mansion – in our Father's house (John 14:2). The person now discovers a staircase in the form of a spiritual teaching or organization. The teaching presents a series of smaller steps that allows the person to ascend to the next floor.

When the person arrives at that floor, he or she will feel as if an entirely new world has opened up. Naturally, most people will want to explore this floor, and there is nothing wrong with taking some time to enjoy the features on this new level of the path. Unfortunately, some people fall into the trap of thinking they have reached the top floor and that there is nothing beyond it. If only they stay on that floor for the rest of their lives, some magic will occur that will lift them to Heaven in one giant leap. They have now closed their minds to the existence of a path that leads from floor to floor until they reach Heaven by their own efforts. The dream that a particular outer organization or philosophy can guarantee your entry into

Heaven is precisely what is described in the saying: "There is a way which seemeth right unto a man, but the end thereof are the ways of death" (Proverbs 14:12).

One aspect of the key of knowledge is that you can never stop searching for a higher understanding. My Father's house has many mansions, or many floors. You can enjoy the features on a particular floor for a time, but there will come a point when you need to look for the staircase that leads to the next floor. If you do not, you will begin to follow the false path to salvation, and it simply cannot lead to Christ consciousness. It will gradually cause you to sink back into self-centeredness and reenter the School of Hard Knocks.

The lawyers had taken away the key of knowledge because they refused to leave the floor on which they were comfortable. They also attempted to prevent other people from finding the staircase to the next floor. When I appeared 2,000 years ago, the lawyers were the leaders of the Jewish religion. They were not willing to look at the new spiritual teaching that God sent me to give to humankind, and they were using their positions of power to prevent others from embracing my teachings. In today's world, you can find such "lawyers" in all areas of society. Some of them are found in the halls of science, and they deny the validity of the spiritual side of life and try to get other people to deny God's existence. Others are found in orthodox religions, and they promote the idea that their religion is the only road to salvation and that all nonbelievers will go to hell. Sadly, many of these modern-day lawyers occupy leadership positions in Christian churches. You even find lawyers in some New Age religions that have already calcified into the belief that they have a monopoly on the key of knowledge.

Let me make a very clear statement. The key of knowledge can never be monopolized by any person, doctrine or organization—and I mean never! No human authority will ever attain a monopoly on truth. The reason being that you can never find or define truth in an outer teaching or doctrine. You can find truth in only one place, namely in God's kingdom. Where is the kingdom of God? Remember one of my most important statements: "The kingdom of God is within you" (Luke 17:21).

### Why do so many churches claim that they have the only truth and that all other religions are false?

Because they want to make you codependent upon the outer organization. They want you to think that the key to salvation is the outer religion. This is the dream of an automatic salvation, which makes people think that by being a member of the right church and by blindly believing its doctrines, God simply has to save them. Yet God is no respecter of persons (Acts 10:34) or the institutions created by persons. No church can guarantee your salvation because the key to salvation is the Christ consciousness. The key to attaining that state of consciousness is found inside yourself.

I challenged the religious authorities of my time because they had turned the Jewish religion into an outer religion that promised a guaranteed path to salvation. They had made most people believe that they could enter Heaven only by going through the outer religion. That is why they were so disturbed when I stated that the kingdom of God is within—meaning that the key to salvation is found inside yourself and not in the outer religion. If most of the Jews had accepted the path I came to offer, the Jewish religion would have been replaced, and the authorities would have lost their positions of power. Because they were not willing to walk the staircase that I came to offer, they tried to kill me in order to hold on to their power over the people. You can never allow your search for truth to be confined to an outer framework, no matter what claims are made by the leaders of that belief system. If someone claims to have a monopoly on truth, they demonstrate that they do not know truth. If you are a sincere seeker, why would you want to follow people who demonstrate that they have not found truth? How can they help you find what they do not have?

**If I understand you correctly, you are essentially saying that we have the ability to know truth from a source inside ourselves. I have met many Christians who vehemently denounce that claim. They say that truth is found only in the doctrines of an outer church, such as the Catholic Church, and that it is a fallacy to believe we can know truth on our own.**

My response is that the statement is both true and not true. When a lifestream has descended too far below the level of the Christ consciousness, that person cannot know truth on his own. The soul is now stuck in a lower state of consciousness, what I call the carnal mind or the death consciousness, and it is dominated by the relative opposites of good and evil. These are relative terms, meaning that they are defined by human beings. When you look at history, it is easy to see that different cultures have had different definitions of good and evil. The reality is that the "tree of the knowledge of good and evil" represents a state of consciousness in which human beings define what they believe is true. They can build a world view that is completely out of touch with the reality of God—yet they believe it is the absolute truth.

As long as you are stuck in the duality of the death consciousness, you do not have the ability to see beyond the relative concepts of good and evil. It is true that a person at this level of spiritual growth (or lack of growth) cannot know truth on his own. It is a fallacy to believe that you can, because your ego will simply define a mental image of what it wants to be true, and you will then seek to project that image upon reality. You will look for a belief system that confirms your mental image, and you will reject any idea that contradicts your "truth."

That is why people at this level do need some outer source of truth in order to have a lifeline that can help them gradually rise above the death consciousness. As I said, we of the ascended masters have released many spiritual teachings in order to give people a lifeline that can – and I stress *can* – help them rise above duality. The problem is that some lifestreams are so deeply lost in the death consciousness that they are not willing to rise above it. Many of these lifestreams are trapped in spiritual pride and they think they know better than others, even better than God. As a consequence of this pride, they believe they should be the leaders of society or the leaders of a particular religion.

What happens to many religions is that after the initial founder disappears, the religion becomes dominated by souls who want to use that religion as a tool for attaining power over the population. These are the souls who become the false prophets (Matthew 7:15) that I rebuked numerous times 2,000 years ago. I compared them to whited sepulchres filled with dead men's bones (Matthew 23:27).

All spiritual people should consider the fact that I clearly came to deliver the Jews from oppression. Yet, contrary to the expectations of many, I did not lead the Jews against the Romans. The reason was that I did not consider the Romans to be the primary oppressors of the Jews. The people that were oppressing the Jews were the false leaders of the Jewish religion. They had managed to make people believe that they could reach God only through the outer religion—meaning that they could not know truth on their own. When you realize this fact, all true Christians should be willing to look in the mirror and see that many Christian churches now promote the very same mindset, namely that you cannot know truth from an inner source but that you need an outer doctrine to define truth for you. They should then recognize that the false prophets are still at work today, as they were 2,000 years ago.

When the ascended masters give a spiritual teaching, that teaching does contain a high degree of truth (if it was delivered through a pure messenger). Yet over time, a spiritual teaching is often degraded and perverted in subtle ways. This happens when a teaching is turned into an organized religion that is defined by outer doctrines. If these doctrines are affected by the duality of the death consciousness, they will inevitably become relative truths. Thereby, what started out as a true spiritual teaching can be turned into the way that seems right unto a man, but the ends thereof are the ways of death.

Those who are far below Christ consciousness can benefit from following an outer religion, as long as the religion contains some truth. Yet when you rise to a higher level of inner maturity, you will gradually sharpen your ability to contact the kingdom of God within you. Thereby, you will acquire the ability to receive truth from a source inside yourself—and we will shortly talk more about that source.

While a person is still completely enveloped in the death consciousness, that person cannot know truth on his own. It is beneficial for such a person to follow an outer religion. Yet when a lifestream matures, it will attain the ability to know a truth that is beyond the relative concepts of good and evil. This truth comes from a source that is above and beyond the death consciousness, and therefore it is not relative. When a lifestream reaches the point of being able to know truth, it is essential for that lifestream to use and sharpen its spiritual sight. If you cling to an outer religion, you will inevitable slow down or stop your spiritual growth.

One might say that for some lifestreams it is right to cling to the outer doctrines of orthodox Christianity because they are not able to recognize a higher truth. Yet for the lifestreams who are open to this book, it is essential to sharpen the ability to know truth from an inner source. This ability is an essential part of attaining Christ consciousness, and there is a double meaning in my statement: "I am the way, the truth, and the life: no man cometh unto the Father, but by me" (John 16:6). One valid interpretation is that no one comes to the kingdom of Heaven without putting on the Christ consciousness. When you do attain the Christ consciousness, you no longer rely on outer doctrines to tell you what is true—that is why I constantly challenged the doctrines of the Jewish religion. Instead, you know truth directly from the source of truth, namely the kingdom of God within you.

**You said that because humankind has reached a higher level of understanding, you can tell us more today than you could 2,000 years ago. Isn't that another reason never to confine our search to a particular belief system?**

That is very true, especially if that belief system has become rigid and dogmatic, meaning that it is no longer open to progressive revelation from Above. Let me explain the central problem on planet earth.

I said that most people have descended into a state of consciousness in which they see themselves as separated from their spiritual source or have forgotten their identity. One might say that the central problem on this planet is ignorance.

In this state of ignorance people feel alone and abandoned, and even many people who believe in God feel that he has left them alone without help. Nothing could be further from the truth! God has never left people alone, no matter how far they have descended below the level of the Christ consciousness. The problem is that the further people descend in consciousness, the harder it becomes for God to give them spiritual guidance. They simply cannot hear the guidance from an inner source so they can be reached only through an outer teaching. When people started descending in consciousness, God assigned the ascended masters to help people come back home. We are constantly seeking to give people tools for raising their consciousness. As a result of our efforts, and some people's willingness to reach for a higher understanding, humankind has indeed been raised to a higher level of consciousness than seen at any previous time in recorded history.

It should be completely obvious that as the consciousness of humankind is raised, we of the ascended masters can give people a more sophisticated spiritual teaching than we could give in the past. The Old Testament truly is a rather primitive spiritual teaching, and it is literally at the kindergarten level compared to what we can give people today. Yet the greatest challenge we face is that people have a tendency to become emotionally attached to the tools we give them. We give people a new religion in order to set them free and help them rise to the next level, the next floor. Yet some people become attached to that religion and refuse to look beyond it. They condemn themselves to staying at the same floor, even though it is time to once again take to the stairs and rise to a new level. That is why you see many people in today's world who cling to orthodox religious doctrines with a fervor that borders on fanaticism.

It is a major problem for us that the very tools we give people in order to set them free so often become perverted into becoming tools to imprison them even more firmly in the death consciousness. Anyway, before I get carried away, let me get back to the task at hand. For people who are open to the spiritual path, it should not be difficult to see that you must always keep your mind open to a higher understanding of life. Progressive revelation should be an essential element in all religions. You should always be on the lookout for the teacher, as he appears in a new disguise.

### What exactly is the teacher we need to look for?

In the Bible you will find the following promise: "Ask, and it shall be given you; seek, and ye shall find; knock, and it shall be opened unto you: For every one that asketh receiveth; and he that seeketh findeth; and to him that knocketh it shall be opened" (Matthew 7:7-8).

I gave that promise because I knew that one of the laws that guide spiritual growth states that if you seek understanding with an open mind and heart, you will always find that understanding. As mentioned earlier, you can describe this law in the following statement: "When the student is ready, the teacher appears." The meaning is that when a lifestream is ready for a higher understanding, the person will immediately be presented with a way to attain this understanding. The simple fact is that we of the ascended masters never leave any soul alone. I realize that many people feel abandoned by God, but there is always a spiritual teacher at your side, and that teacher is always seeking to give you a teaching that can help you grow spiritually.

**I think many people will say that they have often cried out for answers without ever having any spiritual teacher come to them. I know many people who feel that their prayers aren't answered.**

I realize that many people feel this way, and I feel compassion for them. Yet my role as a spiritual teacher is to help them rise above their pain and connect to their spiritual teachers. The reason so many people feel that their prayers aren't answered is that they are not able to see the teacher or they are not willing to look for him. The key to recognizing the teacher is to realize that he often appears in disguise, and the explanation is simple.

Imagine that you find yourself in a crisis and you cry out to me for help. You might feel that you are caught in circumstances beyond your control and that you had no part in creating your misery. Yet I know that the universe is a mirror, and therefore your current situation is a reflection of your state of consciousness. The only way to help you permanently escape your current limitations is to help you rise to a higher level of consciousness, to a higher level on the spiritual path.

How can I help you rise to a higher level? I can do so only by presenting you with an idea that is above and beyond your current beliefs and knowledge. If I only gave you what you already know, how could that help you improve your situation—given that your situation was created based on your current level of consciousness?

Most people find themselves in a spiritual catch-22. They have boxed themselves in by creating a set of limited circumstances. These circumstances are a reflection of their current state of consciousness, yet the people are not willing to look beyond their current beliefs in order to find a higher understanding that will empower them to improve their circumstances.

As a spiritual teacher, I have absolute respect for the Law of Free Will. I cannot force you to accept a higher understanding of life. I can only wait until you ask for it. When you do ask, I cannot necessarily appear to you in a blinding flash, and I cannot talk to you directly because you cannot hear me. I must seek to direct you and help you find an outer teaching that can help you. I can assure you that when a person asks for guidance, the ascended masters will always find a way to present that person with a teaching that is suited to the person's current level of understanding, meaning that it goes a little bit beyond but not too much beyond. The problem is that many people are not willing to look for this teaching. There are several factors that prevent people from recognizing the spiritual teacher when he comes to them:

• Do not expect the teacher to do all the work for you. I am here to help you learn how to become spiritually self-sufficient. I will show you how to solve your problems; I will not solve those problems for you. The earth is a schoolroom for your lifestream. You are here to learn, and I cannot learn your lessons for you. I can only help you learn your lessons.

• I will not present you with a complete solution to your problems. I will present you with an idea that represents the first step on the staircase that leads to the next floor. It is up to you to take that first step, and when you do, I will show you the next step. If you do not take the first step, I cannot force you. I can only wait until you decide to move. As I explained in my parable about the talents (Matthew 25:14-30), it is up to you to multiply what you are given. When you have been faithful over my first instructions, I will give you further instructions.

• The teaching I give you is always beyond your present knowledge and beliefs—or it would not help you. The catch is that if you are not willing to look beyond your current belief system, you will not recognize my teaching, and you might think I have not answered your prayer.

• I cannot talk to all people directly. Many people are not open to a direct teaching but can hear only an indirect teaching. Yet if you ask for help, I will always send you a person who can give you the idea you need—or I will find other ways to present you with this idea. In many cases, I use a human messenger or book to give you the idea you need. Learn to look for the messenger, even if he appears in a humble disguise. Do not shoot my messenger!

• I cannot give you a teaching that is too far beyond your present beliefs, your current mental box. It is up to you to stretch your mind, to expand the box.

**I have always been presented with the idea I needed when I asked with an open mind. However, I haven't always recognized the messenger so what can we do to become better at recognizing our spiritual teachers?**

Many people in today's world are not able to recognize their spiritual teachers, and that is why we can teach them only through an outer teaching, such as a religion. Unfortunately, religions tend to become dogmatic, and thereby the key of knowledge is lost. When you become consciously aware of the spiritual path, it is essential for you to realize that you must become spiritually self-sufficient—meaning that you must be able to get understanding and direction from a source inside yourself.

When you attain Christ consciousness, you establish a direct connection to your I AM Presence and the mind of God. Through this connection, you can get most of the answers you need so you are no longer dependent upon an outer spiritual teaching. Until then, you can still get direction from a source inside yourself, and it comes in the form of an intuitive flash.  Yet for most people it will be highly beneficial to use an outer teaching as a tool for triggering such intuitive flashes.

In India you find the proverb: "The knowledge that is in the books, stays in the books." In reality, this book can do nothing for you. It can give you an intellectual understanding of the spiritual path, but this analytical knowledge will not empower you to change your life. To produce change, knowledge must be internalized. As an example, imagine that you are driving down the road and approach a road sign. You do not need to consciously decide that because you know you have learned to read, you will be able to read the sign. The skill of reading has become so fully integrated in your being that you automatically read the sign without consciously deciding to do so.

I can give you knowledge in this book, but until it is integrated, it will not empower you to move forward on the path. To be integrated, you must use the knowledge in this book as a tool for producing intuitive experiences. If you read this book  with an open mind, certain ideas will ring true in your heart, and this will trigger an intuitive flash that might give you a personalized understanding of the idea. Those ideas will then be integrated into your being. These ideas will be reflected back to you by a higher part of your mind, and they will be expressed in a language that appeals to you. As another example, look at science.

Science is normally a very analytical activity that uses the human intellect. Yet some of the greatest scientific breakthroughs have happened as the result of intuitive experiences. The reason is that the analytical mind – often called the left brain – cannot help you make a conceptual leap. It can help you analyze and make better use of knowledge you already have, but it cannot help you discover knowledge that is outside your current belief system. To transcend your current beliefs, you need to use imagination; what is often called the right brain.

The essence of the spiritual path is to attain a higher state of consciousness, meaning that you move vertically. The analytical mind helps you increase your knowledge of a particular topic, yet that is horizontal knowledge. We might say that analytical knowledge helps you understand and use the features found on your current floor of our Father's house. Yet to find the staircase that leads to the next floor, you need to use your intuition. That is why you see so many people who get stuck in intellectual analysis of spiritual concepts. A perfect example is the many Christian theologians who spend a lifetime studying church history and doctrines. They know every letter of the outer law, as did the Pharisees and the scribes that I rebuked (Matthew 5:20). They have used their intellects to increase their knowledge of God's law, yet they have not used their intuition to discover the Spirit of Truth that is hiding behind the outer law. They have the dead letter, but not the Living Truth (2Corinthians 3:6).

### What is the key to discovering this inner knowledge?

The key is to realize that true knowledge comes from within as the Living Word, the Living Truth. To find it, you must establish a vertical connection, an intuitive connection, to a higher part of your mind, which I like to call your Christ self.

So far I have talked about your conscious self and your I AM Presence. When your lifestream descended into a lower state of consciousness, you lost the conscious connection to your spiritual self. Until you reach some degree of Christ consciousness, you cannot regain that connection. Your I AM Presence resides in the spiritual realm, which is made of much higher vibrations than the material universe. Most people cannot directly perceive those vibrations, and therefore they cannot hear their spiritual selves.

Once again, God has not left you comfortless. He has sent you a mediator in the form of your Christ self. You can look at this as a spiritual teacher – some call it your guardian angel – who is assigned to help you reestablish your connection to your I AM Presence and eventually attain complete oneness with your Presence. The key to your progress on the spiritual path is to increase your conscious connection to your Christ self. The good news is that if you are consciously aware of the spiritual path – and if you weren't, you wouldn't be reading this book – you have already established some connection to your Christ self. You simply need to keep expanding that connection, until you can let this mind be in you, which was also in Christ Jesus (Philippians 2:5).

Many people hear their Christ selves as the "still, small voice within." This is not the voice of conscience that projects guilt or fear into your mind. It is an inner knowing that something is true, even though you might not be able to give an intellectual explanation for why it is true. It can also be a stronger voice that warns you about danger or gives you an unmistakable direction. Most people who are open to this book will find that they have always had this inner voice. They simply need to learn how to use it more consciously.

**Are there any practical tools we can use?**

The main tool is to develop a listening ear whereby you always have some part of your attention directed within. Intuition comes through your heart center or heart chakra, which is located in the center of your chest at the same height as your physical heart. You simply need to realize that your Christ self and your spiritual teachers are always trying to give you understanding and direction. Sometimes you get it from within, and sometimes you get it from without. For example, most people have experienced suddenly finding a book and reading an idea that stands out in their minds as carrying a message they need. Or a person suddenly appears in your life and gives you a message that rings true. As you grow on the path, you will have more of such meaningful "coincidences," and you can gradually become better at recognizing them. You eventually get to the point where you have fully integrated the fact that every situation is an opportunity to learn. You look for the hidden message, and you look for the teacher in disguise.

Another important point is that you develop the willingness to look beyond your current knowledge and beliefs. You never allow any outer belief system to prevent you from finding a higher truth. You recognize the fact that when you make yourself ready by opening your mind to a higher understanding of a specific topic, the teacher will always appear. I give some practical tools for increasing intuition in *The Mystical Teachings of Jesus* and on the website *www.transcendencetoolbox.com*.

# 4 | TAKE CONTROL OF YOUR LIFE

**You talked about the two Rs, namely Revelation and Ritual. My own experience confirms that it is essential to increase our communication with our Christ selves and our spiritual teachers. For me, it has always been intuitive insights that helped me overcome a particular obstacle on the path.**

**Yet I have had times when I felt I had very little intuitive connection. I have met many people who are so overwhelmed by difficult circumstances or their own psychological challenges that they have no attention left over for inner communion. How can such people get on a positive track?**

You don't necessarily need inner communion with your Christ self to start improving your life. In many cases, even an outer, somewhat intellectual, understanding can be enough to get you on a positive track. I fully understand that many people are burdened by a variety of inner and outer circumstances, and therefore they simply cannot establish a clear intuitive connection. Yet they can still acquire an outer understanding that helps them see why they feel like they have lost control over their lives. The brutal fact is that if you are not in control of your life, you are being controlled by somebody or something. Once you see what has taken over your life, you will begin to understand what you can do to take back control of your life.

The essential fact that every spiritual seeker needs to understand is that planet earth is a treacherous environment. This planet has numerous conditions that are in direct opposition to your spiritual growth. Unfortunately, neither mainstream Christianity nor materialistic science can tell people about these forces, and very few people have grown up with an understanding of the factors that oppose their spiritual growth.

It would be helpful for people to have a healthy dose of realism and humility. From my perspective as a spiritual teacher, the current civilization is not nearly as sophisticated as most people like to think. Most people's understanding of the spiritual side of life is as primitive as was people's understanding of physical reality before the discovery of bacteria. Think back to the situation people faced before they knew about bacteria. Many deadly diseases had no known cause and seemed mysterious and frightening. The reality was that people lived in an environment in which they were surrounded by harmful bacteria that could enter their physical bodies through a minor cut, poor hygiene or impure food and water. Yet because people were unaware of this, they had no way to defend themselves against disease. Once people discovered bacteria and understood how they cause disease, they could instantly begin to defend themselves. This has caused many previously fatal diseases to be eradicated or reduced to being easily curable.

Likewise, when people begin to understand what opposes their spiritual growth, it will be easy for them to defend themselves and take back control over their lives. It will require an effort, but for those who are willing, it is possible to build a spiritual defense against any threat to your growth. It will be helpful to begin by contemplating the concept that you live in an environment in which you are surrounded by forces that oppose your spiritual growth. As bacteria can enter your physical body, these forces can enter your spiritual "body" and cause numerous problems. When people feel like they have lost control over their outer situations or over their own psyches, the reason is always that their spiritual bodies have been invaded by certain energies or forces.

I realize this idea can seem somewhat frightening at first, but a bit of thinking will help most people put aside this fear. If you think back to your childhood, you might remember that at a certain age you were taught about bacteria and the need to wash your hands. For some children the idea that there are invisible entities that can kill them is quite frightening. Many children go through a phase of becoming overly concerned about bacteria, perhaps to the point of washing their hands many times a day. Yet, after a while, the mind adjusts, and from now on people simply follow basic hygienic rules without even thinking about it. The new knowledge has now become internalized and is acted upon without fear. When you know how to protect yourself from a danger, you no longer need to fear that danger. This is equally true of spiritual dangers.

Any spiritual seeker needs to increase his or her awareness of the fact that there are a number of spiritual dangers on this planet. Once you understand how these forces can affect you, you will instantly see how you can defend yourself.

**When I first heard about spiritual dangers, it did seem quite frightening. But I soon started feeling a sense of relief, and the reason was that I had intuitively sensed these dangers from early childhood. As a young child I was very afraid of ghosts and supernatural forces, and the reason was that I had an ability to sense the presence of dark energies. I knew these forces existed, but because I didn't understand how to protect myself, I felt very vulnerable. As soon as I started realizing I could protect myself, it was an enormous sense of relief.**

Your experience is quite common among people who are open to the spiritual path, and the explanation is simple. This sensitivity to dark energies goes with the territory.

As I explained earlier, many people have descended far below the level of the Christ consciousness. The farther you descend, the more ego-centered you become, and one effect is that you become less sensitive to the pain and suffering of other people. Yet at the same time you also become less sensitive to anything beyond the material universe. Your experience of reality becomes confined to the physical senses. That is why such people believe there is nothing beyond the material world, and they will vehemently deny the existence of spiritual dangers.

As you grow toward a higher level of consciousness, you regain your original sensitivity to life. As part of this process, your inner faculties will be sharpened, and this is what some people call psychic abilities. The most valuable inner faculty is intuition, and part of it is a sensitivity to energies beyond the material world. This ability allows you to sense, and in some cases see, energies that vibrate at higher or lower frequencies than visible light. Many spiritually-minded people can sense both lower energies and higher energies.

It is often this sensitivity that opens people to the spiritual path and enables them to sense a higher truth. However, the other side of the coin is that you can also sense darker energies. Most people don't have one without the other. I realize that many Christians will frown at this idea, but I actually taught my disciples about this and also taught them how to increase their ability to discern the spirits (1John 4:1). This discernment of spirits includes the ability to sense lower and higher energies. You can know the difference between spirits/energies of light and darkness.

**It is a natural part of spiritual growth that we increase our ability to sense spiritual dangers? I sometimes wondered whether I was more vulnerable to such energies than the average person?**

On the contrary. Because you sensed the lower energies and also sensed higher energies, you were actually less vulnerable. You will see that your sensitivity often enabled you to avoid certain situations that your peers rushed into blindly. I realize that some people claim ignorance is bliss, but that is simply not true. The millions of people who died from bacterial infections might have felt secure, but their ignorance was not blissful—it was lethal.

However, because you could sense darker energies, you naturally felt more vulnerable to them than people who did not have this sensitivity. I realize this caused you a lot of fear during your childhood, but the reason was that you grew up in a culture that did not teach you how to protect yourself from dark energies. Once you understand how to protect yourself and start applying such protection, your sense of vulnerability fades—wouldn't you agree?

**Absolutely! Learning how to use spiritual protection has been one of the greatest gifts I have received as a result of discovering the spiritual path. It made an incredible difference in my sense of peace and my ability to enjoy life. I am a totally different person today than I was before I knew how to invoke spiritual protection.** *[Note: To learn more about spiritual protection and find techniques for protecting yourself, study the website www.transcendencetoolbox.com.]*

One of the most important concepts on the spiritual path is the idea that what one human being has done, all can do. With that in mind, let us move on and consider how people can learn to protect themselves against the forces that oppose their spiritual growth.

The first factor we need to talk about is the fact that everything is energy, and therefore everything you do is done with energy. Consequently, every aspect of your life is affected by the natural laws that define how energy works. If you are serious about spiritual growth, it is absolutely essential that you attain a greater understanding of how energy works. We have already described this in great detail in *The Power of Self* and other books. I will simply give an overview in this book so that people who have not yet read the other books can understand the big picture. The topic of energy should be studied by all spiritual seekers until the knowledge of how to use energy becomes fully integrated. For example, protecting yourself from toxic energy should be as automatic as protecting your body from harmful bacteria.

The concept that everything is energy is a perfect example of why progressive revelation is necessary. When I taught my disciples 2,000 years ago, it was impossible for me to explain how energy affects your life. The discoveries of science have given me much better options for helping people attain a higher understanding of this important aspect of spiritual growth.

Let us begin by contemplating how people can adjust their world view based on the fact that everything is made from energy. You might remember that I explained how attaining Christ consciousness moves you out of a state of mind dominated by duality and into a sense of oneness. When Albert Einstein discovered that everything is energy, he made it much easier for humankind to escape duality and begin to see the underlying oneness. Unfortunately, most people have not changed their world view based on Einstein's findings, but that should not stop a spiritual seeker.

The fact that everything is made from energy means that there are no barriers in the universe. Traditionally, religious people have seen a barrier between Heaven and earth, but it was never real. The material world and the spiritual world are both made from energy, and the only difference between them is a difference in the vibration of the energy waves. There truly is no barrier, and this is what allows you to receive directions and energy from the spiritual realm. The human mind works like a radio. When you are stuck in duality, your personal radio can receive only one station, namely the material universe that you can detect with the physical senses. As you climb toward Christ consciousness, you build a bigger antenna, and you can now receive more stations. This is what makes spiritual growth possible.

Another barrier that was never real is the barrier between mind and matter. Einstein's discovery proved that solid matter is made from energy, and since thoughts are clearly a form of energy, it is possible that thoughts can influence matter. This explains why human beings have created the suffering you currently see on earth. They have done this through the power of their minds, and we will later explore how.

For now, the important concept is that there is no barrier between the spiritual and the material worlds. The material universe is an extension of the spiritual world, and we might compare the physical universe to the tip of an iceberg. It is part of a larger whole, but as long as people are trapped in the consciousness of duality, they cannot perceive the spiritual realm. It is hidden from view, as most of an iceberg is under water.

As you climb the spiritual path, you increase your sensitivity to energies beyond the material realm, and that should make it easy for people to accept that they are more than their physical bodies. You know that a magnet has an invisible field around it, and your body also has an energy field around it. In reality, the totality of your being is an energy field, and the physical body is simply the densest part of that energy field. It is important for spiritual seekers to contemplate the fact that they have an energy field around their bodies. All other people also have such fields so when you interact with another person, there is more to the interaction than meets the eye. All human interactions involve an exchange of invisible, what we might call psychic, energy. I think everyone has experienced being yelled at by someone who is angry and then feeling down afterward. The reason is that an angry person sends out low-frequency, toxic energy that enters your field and affects how you feel and think about yourself.

Based on these straightforward considerations, it should be obvious to anyone that if you are serious about spiritual progress, it is essential that you learn how to protect your personal energy field against being invaded by toxic energy from outside sources. When you know how energy works, it becomes easy to see how to protect yourself.

Energy is simply vibration, and when a person engages in a negative feeling, such as anger, that person is sending out energy waves of a certain frequency. It should be obvious that anger will produce energy waves of a lower frequency than a positive emotion, such as love. Science can tell you that energy waves of a lower frequency cannot penetrate waves of a higher frequency. This is illustrated in many science fiction movies where a spaceship has a protective shield around it that neither missiles nor laser beams can penetrate.

It now becomes obvious that one way to protect your energy field is to create a protective shield around it. This shield must be made from energy of higher frequencies than the many forms of toxic energies found on planet earth. Where is the natural place to find such frequencies? Obviously, it is the spiritual realm, which is made from vibrations that are higher than any of the vibrations in the material world. If you invoke a shield of high-frequency spiritual energy around your personal energy field, it can literally protect you against any of the vibrations found in the material world. If the protective shield is strong enough, you will be invulnerable to any toxic energies.

**That is such an obvious idea, and it blows my mind that more people haven't understood this concept. I mean, this one idea could have a major impact on people's lives and their spiritual growth. I think this concept should be taught to people in kindergarten.**

One day it will be, but until then it will be up to people to learn it on their own.

### How can we best invoke spiritual protection?

It all starts with the recognition that invoking spiritual protection does not require any kind of magic or supernatural abilities. You already have everything you need because your lifestream was designed as a conduit through which spiritual energy can stream into the material world.

The material universe can continue to exist only because there is a constant stream of spiritual energy flowing into this world from a higher realm. However, the flow of this energy is not simply a mechanical process. The energy can flow only through the minds of self-aware beings. Some of these beings reside in the spiritual realm, and we are the ascended masters. Part of our mission is to direct spiritual energy and to step it down in vibration until it can be received by human beings in embodiment.

It is important for people to consider the statement: "And God said, Let us make man in our image, after our likeness" (Genesis 1:26). One aspect of this is that human beings have the ability to let spiritual energy stream through their minds. They can then direct that energy and they can lower the vibration of the energy. You already have a built-in ability to invoke high-frequency spiritual energy, to let it stream through your mind and to direct it into forming a protective shield around your personal energy field.

Throughout history, the ascended masters have given people many different techniques for invoking and directing spiritual energy. Most religious rituals were originally given as such techniques. Yet because people did not have an understanding of energy, the original purpose for the rituals was rarely understood. Consequently many rituals have been perverted, forgotten or have been used in a rote manner that did not have the desired effect. To get the best effect from using a spiritual technique, you need the following:

• You need an inner connection to your Christ self and through that to the spiritual realm. Most people already have some connection. Yet the stronger the connection becomes – the more your heart is into performing the ritual – the more energy you can invoke. Your connection is the open door, and the wider the door, the more energy can stream through it.

• After invoking a stream of energy, you need to direct it into specific situations. You do this with your conscious mind. This involves vision and willpower. The more you understand about life and your own psychology, the better you can direct spiritual energy into specific situations. For example, the more you understand about the forces that oppose your progress, the better you can build your spiritual defense—and the more determined you will be in terms of maintaining that defense.

• After invoking energy and deciding where to direct it, you need to build a momentum that will conquer the forces that oppose your progress. You need persistence, but you also need to find a technique that gives you the best possible results.

Although there are many techniques available, they can basically be divided into two categories. Some techniques, such as meditation and contemplation, help you go within and establish or reinforce your connection to the spiritual realm. These techniques can help you open up the flow of energy, but you will not get the maximum benefit unless you also employ techniques for directing the energy and building momentum. Visualization techniques can help you direct the energy, but the best way to build an irresistible momentum is to use the power of the spoken word.

There is an important message in the quote: "And God said, Let there be light: and there was light" (Genesis 1:3). The fact is that God used the power of the word, the power of sound, to create the material universe. The most effective rituals for invoking spiritual protection use the spoken word. This can be anything from chants, as used in the East or in Gregorian chants, to spoken prayers, affirmations, decrees or rosaries.

The most efficient ritual for invoking spiritual protection that is currently available on this planet is the decrees and invocations to Archangel Michael. [See *www.transcendencetoolbox.com*.] They are specifically designed to protect you from any of the forces that oppose your spiritual progress. Archangel Michael is a very powerful spiritual being who is assigned by God to protect your faith, your life and your spiritual progress from the forces of this world. For anyone serious about spiritual progress, it will be extremely beneficial to invoke the Presence of Archangel Michael in their lives.

**I can attest to the power of invoking Archangel Michael's protection, as I have been doing since 1984. Before that time, I often felt greatly burdened by psychic or dark energies, and I was especially sensitive to toxic energy from other people. By invoking Archangel Michael, I have risen above that and feel like I have much more control over my emotions and my thoughts.**

**In the beginning, I invoked spiritual protection in a somewhat mechanical manner, and I didn't feel I had the inner connection you are talking about. I didn't really know how to direct the energy either, but I still feel it had a beneficial effect. What would you recommend for people who feel overwhelmed by toxic energy and have little intuitive connection?**

For such people it is essential to use the most efficient tools possible, and that is why they need the spoken word. I know that many spiritual seekers have used meditation, yoga or visualization, but such tools require a strong inner connection to be effective. The spoken word, especially decrees to Archangel Michael, will have a powerful effect even if you have little inner connection and do not use much visualization. That is why the spoken word is the best way to overcome the sense of being overwhelmed. As you get your head above the water – or rather the toxic energies pulling you down – you can begin to build your inner connection and your power to visualize. This will increase the efficiency of your spoken prayer, and it will also make it more feasible for you to use meditation and visualization.

**As you know, I used meditation for a couple of years before I heard about the spoken word, and I actually felt that mediation opened me up to lower energies. Is that true, and if so how does that happen?**

When you look at history, it should be obvious that humankind has generated an enormous amount of toxic energy that is floating around in the energy field of the planet. This energy will naturally accumulate because like attracts like. As the

accumulation intensifies, the energy will begin to form vortexes, much like a maelstrom in the ocean. Such vortexes can
overpower your thoughts and emotions. What has happened
over the past several decades is that millions of people in the
West have become more interested in spiritual growth. Because
neither mainstream Christianity nor science could satisfy these
people's spiritual longing, many of them have looked to the
East to find spiritual teachings and techniques.

Please don't misunderstand me. The East has many wonderful teachings and techniques, and I studied and used some
of them when I traveled in the East during my "lost" years. Yet
there are a couple of problems with uncritically transferring
Eastern teachings to people in the West. First of all, Eastern
people are naturally more spiritually minded whereas Western
people are more practical. That is why many Eastern techniques focus on opening the connection to the spiritual realm.
Yet spiritual seekers in the West really need techniques that
can help them direct spiritual energy into creating concrete
changes in their lives and on the planet.

In the West most people are more active and outgoing, and
they often live more busy lives. The upside is that the West
has a higher standard of living and is better at taking care of
people's material needs. The downside is that many areas in
the West, especially large cities, have intense vortexes of toxic
energies, which many sensitive people experience as stress.
When people live busy lives in a highly stressful environment,
their minds are often filled with thoughts that are somewhat
chaotic. It therefore seems very appealing to use a form of
Eastern meditation that is designed to calm the mind and possibly empty it of all thoughts.

The problem is that while people are in their normal state
of consciousness, their conscious minds can keep out at least
some of the toxic energy – and stress-filled thoughts – in the

environment. When you empty the mind of thoughts, you can easily remove this form of defense, and many Western people have no defense left. Their energy fields now become open to the toxic energies and impure thoughts in their environment and they are often overwhelmed by it. That is why some people, such as yourself, initially feel a great calming effect from meditation but later begin to feel agitated when meditating.

I am not hereby saying that people need to give up meditation or other Eastern techniques. However, they need to realize that most Eastern techniques were meant to be given to people who lived in the protected environment of a retreat or ashram. Some techniques are so powerful that they were given only by a personal guru who could oversee the effects on the student. When you uncritically give such techniques to anyone, you will have some people who open their minds to lower energies. The key to overcoming this problem is to apply an efficient technique for spiritual protection so you can seal yourself from the toxic energies and impure thoughts in your environment. If people would combine spiritual protection with their meditation, most of them would get better results from meditation.

**I actually had to give up meditating for years. Yet when I started invoking spiritual protection, I could meditate again without being overwhelmed by energy. You mentioned that we could also be disturbed by toxic energy in our own energy fields. What can we do to free ourselves from this problem?**

As we talked about earlier, there is a constant stream of energy flowing through your mind from your I AM Presence. Your mind changes the vibration of the energy, and science has proven that once an energy wave has taken on a certain vibration, it will stay in that vibration indefinitely. It should not be difficult for people to envision that as they go through a traumatic experience, their thoughts and emotions are producing energy waves of a certain frequency. Even when you no longer feel anger, the energy you produced will not simply vanish into thin air. Some of it will be sent into the universe, and it will be reflected back to you by the cosmic mirror. Yet some of the energy will be stored in your personal energy field.

Over a lifetime, you can accumulate a substantial amount of low-frequency energy in your field. You know that the earth exerts a gravitational pull on your body because like attracts like. The toxic energy stored in your energy field will exert a pull on your psychic body, meaning your subconscious and conscious minds. The accumulated psychic energy can interfere with your conscious thoughts and feelings. The accumulated energy can form a vortex in your field that overpowers your conscious mind.

Imagine that you have created a vortex of anger in your energy field. The magnetic pull of this energy will influence your ability to respond to various situations. When you experience a situation that does not follow your expectations, the magnetic pull will increase the likelihood that you respond to the situation with anger. As the accumulation of psychic energy increases, the magnetic pull can eventually become so strong that you lose control over your conscious mind. You are no longer able to consciously choose your reaction to certain situations. Your reactions are predetermined because the energy in your field overpowers your conscious willpower.

That is why you see people who cannot control their anger no matter how hard they try. If you are serious about walking the spiritual path, you need to take control over your energy field. You have to prevent the accumulation of negative psychic energy in your field. If such energy has already accumulated, as it has for most people, you have to find a way to remove the energy.

Obviously, an important part of this is to stop yourself from creating more toxic energy. As the energy from your spiritual self passes through your subconscious and conscious minds, it will take on the vibrations of your beliefs and your attitudes about life. If you have a negative attitude toward life, you will lower the vibration of the energy from your spiritual self.

There is meant to be a natural flow of energy from your spiritual self to your lower being and back to your spiritual self. The energy can flow back to your spiritual self only if it has a high enough vibration, meaning that it is qualified with the vibration of love. The energy that flows back to your I AM Presence becomes your treasure laid up in Heaven (Matthew 6:20), but it will also be multiplied and sent back to you in greater measure, as I explained in my parable about the talents (Matthew 25:14-30). You need to avoid misqualifying the energy that streams from your I AM Presence by learning how to avoid responding to situations with negative feelings. This will require you to resolve some of the emotional wounds that you have received, and we can talk about that in greater detail later.

Another important factor is to learn how to transform the low-frequency energy that has already accumulated in your personal energy field. This can be done by invoking high-frequency spiritual energy and directing it into the low-frequency energy. As scientists have demonstrated, if you direct a high-frequency energy wave at a low-frequency energy wave, you can actually raise the vibration of the low-frequency wave.

You can invoke such transforming energy the same way you invoke spiritual protection, only you need to invoke a different type of spiritual energy. The color of Archangel Michael's spiritual light is a very intense, pulsating electric blue color. The most efficient form of energy for transforming toxic energy has an electric violet color. Violet has the highest vibration of the visible colors, and the spiritual energy I am talking about has a vibration very close to the material spectrum. It is very efficient in terms of transforming accumulated psychic energy.

As I explain in *The Mystical Teachings of Jesus*, the ascended masters have, since the 1930s, been permitted to release several techniques for invoking this violet energy—often called the Violet Flame. This is a major dispensation because in prior ages the use of this energy was not taught to the public. Yet because humankind has risen to a higher level of consciousness, it was decided to publicly release techniques for invoking the Violet Flame. This is done with the hope that people will no longer seek to misuse this energy. We have released special decrees and Mother Mary has released a series of invocations that invoke the Violet Flame [See *www.transcendencetoolbox. com*].

We earlier talked about people who feel overwhelmed by life, and we can now see that this feeling is caused by low-frequency psychic energy. Some of this energy enters your field from the outside and some of it you produce internally. By applying the two-prong approach of invoking spiritual protection and invoking the Violet Flame for the transmutation of accumulated energy, most people will quickly notice an improvement. They will begin to feel less overwhelmed and will gradually regain control of their lives.

I understand that when people feel overwhelmed, applying a spiritual technique might seem beyond their capability. Yet most people routinely make certain efforts to protect their bodies from harmful bacteria or chemical substances. It is not difficult to learn how to protect your mind from negative psychic energy.

By making a small, but determined, effort, most people will quickly begin to feel like they have more energy, and eventually they will begin to feel a greater sense of peace of mind.

**I can certainly witness to that. Back in 1984, I started invoking protection and the Violet Flame. I had certain situations from my teenage years that would often haunt me and make me feel emotional pain. After I had invoked the Violet Flame every day for 3-4 months, I suddenly realized that I could now think about these situations without feeling the same intensity of emotional pain.**

**I had done nothing else to change this condition so I can only attribute it to the fact that, by invoking the Violet Flame, I had removed some of the accumulated energy in my field. There was no longer the same magnetic pull on my emotions. Since then, I have experienced even more dramatic effects from invoking the violet flame energy.**

You are correct, and most people will experience similar results. However, it is important for people to realize that it will take time to transmute all of the toxic energy in their fields. This energy has accumulated over a long period of time so it cannot all be resolved in a matter of days or months.

Many people will experience a relatively dramatic effect after a short period of time, and the reason is that you can quickly remove some of the less dense energy. Because you feel the contrast between before and after, you experience it as a dramatic shift. Yet as you continue to invoke violet flame energy, you will go deeper into the psyche and begin to deal with some of the denser energies. It will take longer to work through the energies and you will experience a more gradual progress that is easy to overlook.

**I can also witness to that. I have had periods where I felt like I wasn't making any progress. Sometimes I had to call for the transmutation of a particular problem for years before I saw results. Yet the results have always been there. I also have to say that even though I have been invoking spiritual energy since 1984 by using other techniques, I have noticed a definite acceleration from using the new decrees and invocations.**

The reason is that Mother Mary's invocations not only invoke violet flame energy but also help you resolve some of the imperfect beliefs and attitudes that cause you to continue to misqualify energy. You get a double effect from these calls, and that is why Mother Mary calls them the most powerful spiritual rituals on the planet. I strongly encourage all sincere spiritual seekers to apply these invocations and keep using them indefinitely. Obviously, some people might need more time to see dramatic results, but by remaining constant in the invocation of spiritual energy, all people will eventually see results that are unmistakable.

I can assure you that the release of these decrees and invocations represents a major step forward for spiritual seekers. In today's world you have better tools than at any time in recorded history. Quite frankly, I find it difficult to see how any sincere seeker could ignore or reject these tools.

**·d you go so far as to say that you cannot make mum progress on the spiritual path without**

**applying an efficient tool for spiritual protection and for transforming toxic energy?**

I will. Why not make use of the techniques that are available in today's world? Refusing to do so would be like continuing to use candles instead of electricity.

**What about selecting a tool. Is this an individual thing, or do you think everyone should apply the tools you recommend?**

Obviously, it is an individual matter and people need to find a tool that applies to them at their present level of consciousness. However, people who are open to this book should seriously consider using the tools I am recommending here. When the student is ready, the teacher appears. If you have found this book, it can only be because you are ready for the teachings and the tools it can give you.

**Many people in the West like tools such as yoga and meditation. Can they still make progress without using the decrees and invocations you mentioned?**

Sure, but the question is how quickly they progress. Imagine that you are going to a faraway destination and you have the choice between a bicycle and a car. Both will get you there so you simply need to decide how quickly you want to arrive at the destination. I am not saying people necessarily need to give up the tools they have been using. I am saying that by using the decrees and invocations to invoke spiritual protection and the transformation of toxic energy, the effects of other spiritual tools will be magnified dramatically. Again, why not make use of the tools that are available in this age?

# 5 | LEAVE IT BEHIND

**As I mentioned in the introduction, I got some negative reactions from my family when I started walking the spiritual path, and I know many other people who have had similar experiences. Can you help us understand why that happens to us?**

I can, and let us begin by acknowledging that this is an extremely important point that all spiritual seekers will benefit from understanding. As I said earlier, human beings have descended into a state of consciousness that is dominated by duality, such as the opposites of relative good and evil or action and reaction. One might say that when lifestreams descended into the dualistic consciousness, they fell into a realm of denser energies in which everything is dominated by a set of natural laws that are lower than, subservient to, the spiritual laws operating in higher realms.

The law of action and reaction demonstrates that, in this world, everything comes with a price. Whatever you choose has an effect, and the effect might limit your freedom to make choices in the future. A simple yet profound expression of this principle is the old saying: "You can't have your cake and eat it too." It is extremely important for spiritual seekers to contemplate the deeper meaning behind this seemingly simple statement. The statement holds the key to understanding an essential element of the spiritual path, namely the need to make the choice to leave a limitation behind.

One might say that the spiritual path is a process whereby the lifestream gradually rises to greater and greater levels of creative freedom and expression. In order to rise to a higher level of freedom, the lifestream must be willing to leave behind a certain mental limitation, a limited state of consciousness that is restricting the soul's spiritual freedom. As I have tried to explain with the concept that the universe is a mirror, it is the limitations in your consciousness that are holding you back.

Compare this to the life-cycle of a butterfly. The larva spins a cocoon that sustains it through the winter. When spring arrives, it breaks open the cocoon, folds out its wings and flies toward the sun, leaving the cocoon behind forever. Yet what if the butterfly became emotionally attached to the cocoon and refused to leave it? The butterfly would still be fully developed inside the hardened shell, but it could not fly until it decided to break the shell and unfold its wings. It is much the same with a lifestream on the path.

We might say that all lifestreams have had various unpleasant experiences during their journey on earth. This has caused them to create a cocoon around themselves as a means of protection against the forces of this world. This shell is a limited sense of identity, a limited sense of who you are and what you can do. It is what many people call the soul. Inevitably, this protection limits the lifestream's freedom and creativity so the lifestream is condemned to live in a mental box that might be very small. The essence of the spiritual path is that the lifestream learns to protect itself with spiritual means so that it can gradually overcome its limitations and expand the box of self-awareness, its sense of identity.

I earlier compared the path to a staircase between the floors in a building. When a lifestream explores a particular floor, it is as if the lifestream is growing inside the cocoon. The floor provides a protected environment in which the lifestream can grow for a time. The wings of the lifestream eventually become fully developed, but in order to rise to the next level, the lifestream must be willing to leave behind its protective shell. It is not a matter of somehow transforming this shell. It must be permanently discarded because it has served its purpose and is no longer needed. It must be left behind with no sense of regret or loss. This can often be one of the major stumbling blocks for lifestreams on the path. They become emotionally attached to a limited sense of identity – they become comfortable – and refuse to leave it behind although it is past the time to move on to a higher level.

It is extremely important for spiritual seekers to realize that the path is a process of making choices. Some of those choices require you to leave behind certain limitations in your mind, especially limitations related to how you see yourself and your abilities. One might say that the spiritual path is a process whereby the lifestream gradually fulfills the old axiom: "Man – and woman – know thyself!" As you ascend the path, you leave behind all limitations or falsehoods concerning who you are and what is possible or impossible. However, in order to accept a higher sense of identity, you must permanently leave behind the limited sense of identity.

This process of leaving limitations behind is described in the biblical sayings: "Choose you this day whom ye will serve" (Joshua 24:15) and "Choose life" (Deuteronomy 30:19). I attempted to explain this in further detail in my saying: "No man can serve two masters: for either he will hate the one, and love the other; or else he will hold to the one, and despise the other. Ye cannot serve God and mammon" (Matthew 6:24).

Many Christians have misinterpreted this to mean that when you are a religious person, you need to despise money. In reality, "mammon" does not refer exclusively to money but should be understood as "the things of this world." If you are emotionally attached to the things of this world, it becomes very difficult to follow the spiritual path. This is also explained in my parable about the man who was not willing to leave behind his riches to become one of my disciples (Matthew 19:20-24).

**It really isn't the things in themselves but the attachments to them that hold us back on the path? Having money is not necessarily evil, as many Christians believe, if only you are not attached to the money or anything else in this world?**

That is correct. It truly is the attachment more than the possession of worldly riches that prevents you from growing spiritually. Yet it must be added that when people have great possessions, they often become very attached to them because they could not imagine life without them. Their possessions have become such an integral part of their sense of identity that they think they will lose their identity without the possessions. The greatest fear any lifestream can have is the fear of losing its identity.

People might contemplate the saying: "You can't take it with you." Although the common interpretation is that you can't take your material possessions with you when you die, it also applies to the spiritual path. You can't take your limited sense of identity with you when you ascend to a higher level of the path. The inner meaning of the saying that you cannot serve two masters is that you cannot be in two different states of consciousness at once. You cannot simultaneously identify yourself as a spiritual being, as a son or daughter of God, and as a mortal human being who is a miserable sinner. You must choose which sense of identity you will serve as the master of your life.

Before rising to a new level of the spiritual path, you might go through a phase where you are not quite ready to leave behind a limited sense of identity so you seek to hold on to it a while longer. Yet there will come a moment of truth when it is necessary to make the hard choice of leaving behind a certain limitation. This is a test that comes to all spiritual seekers, and it comes every time you ascend to a higher level; to the next floor. As I explained earlier, you cannot start the spiritual path until you are willing to take responsibility for yourself. Before you can start the path, you must make the choice to leave behind the limited sense of identity that portrays you as a victim of circumstances beyond your control. Only then can you follow the path whereby you raise your consciousness through your own efforts.

**Would it be fair to say that one factor that opposes our spiritual growth is a pressure from outside ourselves to not follow the spiritual path?**

Yes, there is indeed a magnetic pull that seeks to prevent people from ascending the staircase, and it is important to be aware of this. When you know that this force exists, it becomes easier to identify it as it approaches you in disguise. Once you identify what you are up against, it becomes much easier to avoid being fooled by the temptation to stay in a limited state of consciousness.

Carl Jung was one of the first psychologists to talk about a "collective unconscious" as a force that influences all human beings. We might also talk about a mass consciousness, and we can compare it to a vortex of energy that has formed a black hole. This maelstrom is trying to suck every lifestream into it so that no one can escape the gravitational pull and ascend the spiritual path. As there is no light coming out of a black hole, there is no spiritual light coming out of the mass consciousness. Fortunately, it is possible to lessen the downward pull of the mass consciousness, and this has indeed happened over the past several millennia. That is why you see progress in society and in people's spiritual awareness. As I said: "And I, if I be lifted up from the earth, will draw all men unto me" (John 12:32). Likewise, every time one person raises his or her state of consciousness, it will lessen the downward pull of the mass consciousness and make it easier for other people to find and follow the spiritual path.

There are two main pressures that seek to pull you away from the spiritual path. One is what we might call a pull from below, and it comes from your peers, such as family and friends. People who knew you before you became consciously aware of the path have often formed a mental image of who you are and how they want you to live your life. People are often reluctant to let go of these images and allow you to make changes to your lifestyle according to your newfound understanding of the spiritual side of life. This is usually caused by either fear or envy. They either do not want you to leave them behind, or they do not want you to rise above them. Yet, at the same time, some of these people might not be willing to follow you on the spiritual path. The only way they can avoid being left behind is to hold you back and prevent you from walking the path. They are not willing to grow themselves, but they are willing to stop your growth in order to remain where they are comfortable.

This problem is the true message in my saying: "If any man come to me, and hate not his father, and mother, and wife, and children, and brethren, and sisters, yea, and his own life also, he cannot be my disciple" (Luke 14:26). Many people have been baffled by this statement and think it sounds unnecessarily harsh or cruel. Yet the quote in the Bible does not give the entire context of the message. The true context is that if you want to follow the spiritual path, you cannot allow any person to hold you back. In reality, you do not need to hate your family or leave them behind. You simply need to overcome the emotional attachment that makes you feel you should remain subservient to your family, even to the point that you should not walk the spiritual path against their wishes.

It is much like our earlier discussion that it is not possessions but the attachment to possessions that prevents you from growing spiritually. It is not your family or friends, but your attachment to them and their opinion of you that prevents you from growing.

**What can people do to overcome this problem? I mean, some people have had tremendous conflicts and have had to leave behind parents, siblings, spouses or long-term friends. Does it always have to be a conflict or is there a better way to deal with this?**

The universe is a mirror so your relationships with other people will be a reflection of what goes on in your own consciousness. The problem here is that when people first discover the spiritual path, they are usually still caught in a consciousness of duality. This causes them to see things from a more black-and-

white perspective, meaning that people see two polar opposites instead of the Middle Way that transcends the relative
opposites.

When some people discover the spiritual path, they
become very enthusiastic and think it is the most important
aspect of their lives. This is partly due to the fact that society
does not teach people about the path at an early age. When
people finally discover it, they feel as if they have no time to
lose and must devote their lives entirely to the path. This is
not necessarily wrong, however as people mature they usually
become more balanced.

I am quite aware that many people have found the path
and then experienced a seemingly unresolvable conflict with a
family member, such as a spouse. In some cases, such a conflict can be transcended, but because of free will this is not
always possible.

**Let's say you have a spouse who grumpily lets you
follow the spiritual path for a while, but then one
day confronts you and wants you to make a choice
between the path and your spouse. I have known
people who became angry when they realized that
my relationship to God is more important to me than
anything else. They wanted me to set them above
the path and basically give up the path to maintain
a relationship with them. What is your response to
that?**

My response is that the Law of Free Will is the absolute law
for this universe. You have an absolute, God-given right to follow the spiritual path and to value your relationship with God
higher than your relationship with any human being. Unless

you set your priorities this way, you cannot make it to the end of the spiritual path and attain Christ consciousness.

No human being has a right to override your free will. If you are a spiritual person, you have a right to put your spiritual quest before any of the activities of this world, including your relationship with your family. If your family attempts to pressure or persuade you into using your outer mind to override the deeper choice of your lifestream, they are violating the Law of Free Will. They have no right to do so, and consequently you have no obligation to give in to their demands.

Yet this does not necessarily mean that there needs to be an unresolvable conflict between you and your family. Again, your relationships are a reflection of your state of consciousness. At a certain stage of the path, you are still trapped in duality. As long as you see things with the dualistic mind, you will see no resolution to a conflict. Yet it is possible to rise above duality and see that there is a Middle Way.

In that respect, it can be helpful for seekers to study the life of Gautama Buddha. He was born in a royal family and for a time lived in great luxury. He had everything the world has to offer but had no spiritual content in his life. He then discovered the spiritual path and jumped into the opposite extreme, becoming an ascetic living in the forest. Yet after several years of this, he realized it was too extreme, and he then discovered the Middle Way that allows you to grow spiritually without going into the extremes.

When people first discover the path, many of them tend to go from one extreme – a worldly lifestyle – to the opposite extreme of focusing all attention on the path. Yet if people would consider the need to find balance, to find the Middle Way, they could avoid this unbalanced reaction. This could avoid or resolve many conflicts between people and their families.

The key to finding the Middle Way is that you must be absolutely firm in yourself about your priorities in life. You must be resolved that your first priority is the spiritual path. Yet you must be equally resolved that you will do the best you can to also fulfill your worldly responsibilities. When you find this inner resolution, it will help your family members make peace with the fact that you are on the spiritual path. They will respect your choice to be on the path, yet they will not feel threatened by it because they realize you will not leave them behind or neglect them.

I am aware that free will is always a factor. Even if you are resolved in yourself, your spouse can still choose to stay in the all-or-nothing, dualistic frame of mind and demand that you choose him/her over the path. In that case, it can be necessary to leave such a person behind and find your spiritual family rather than your worldly family. This is also illustrated in a story from my life:

> 46 While he yet talked to the people, behold, his mother and his brethren stood without, desiring to speak with him.
> 47 Then one said unto him, Behold, thy mother and thy brethren stand without, desiring to speak with thee.
> 48 But he answered and said unto him that told him, Who is my mother? and who are my brethren?
> 49 And he stretched forth his hand toward his disciples, and said, Behold my mother and my brethren!
> 50 For whosoever shall do the will of my Father which is in Heaven, the same is my brother, and sister, and mother. (Matthew, Chapter 50)

This story illustrates that when you are on the spiritual path, you cannot allow any person to hold you back. If your family attempts to hold you back, you might need to find your spiritual family. Yet you will also see from my life that my mother and some of my brothers did end up joining me on my journey. However, I can assure you that had I not been resolved in myself, they would not have been set free to overcome the force that was working through them, seeking to use them to prevent me from fulfilling my mission.

**Are you saying that we need to approach the path in a balanced way, and the more balanced we can be, the greater the possibility that we will get a balanced reaction from other people?**

Correct. At the beginning phases of the path, a person is often unbalanced and sees everything in terms of the relative opposites of black and white, often labeled right and wrong. This is what causes some religious people to cross the line into fanaticism, and the extreme effect is that they begin to believe God wants them to kill all non-believers. This is what you have seen outplay itself as some of the worst atrocities in history, such as the crusades, the inquisition and today's religiously motivated terrorism.

Fanaticism and extremism have nothing to do with the true spiritual path. They represent the way that seems right unto a man, but the end thereof are the ways of death (Proverbs 14:12). The true spiritual path is the Middle Way of balance in all things. When a person first discovers the path, it often tends to become a bit extreme. Yet by being consciously aware of the need to find balance, you can shorten this period and quickly discover the Middle Way. This can greatly minimize the conflicts you have with family and friends.

The more balanced you are, the less you will stir people's fears of losing you. Many people have generated fear in their families precisely because family members could clearly see that they were following the path in an unbalanced – and often unhealthy – way. This is a legitimate concern and is not necessarily motivated by fear and envy (although such feelings can be mixed in). It is actually the family members who are more balanced. The problem is that people often use a spiritual teaching to convince themselves that because they are on the path, they are right and it is necessary for them to do what they have to do. They reason it is the family members who are unwilling to understand the spiritual path.

The only way out of this impasse is that the person on the path realizes the need for balance and therefore snaps out of the extremist approach to the path. Unfortunately, this often happens only when the person has used a spiritual teaching to box himself in to the point where he can no longer move. The spiritual path is meant to set your lifestream free from its limited sense of identity, its mental box. Yet some people find a spiritual teaching and use it to create a new mental box that is narrower than their previous box. They fanatically follow what they see as the spiritual path until they can no longer stand it. Something finally breaks, and such people often give up on the path. Some of them become bitter and think they were fooled, while others eventually find their way back to the path and a more balanced approach.

It is my hope that this book can help people become aware of this seesaw response so they can avoid falling into this trap of going from one extreme to the other. The path truly is all about balance. The way of extremism is not the true spiritual path because it is based on the relative opposites that spring from the death consciousness. The Middle Way is the way to Christ consciousness because it raises you above relative opposites. It helps you see beyond duality and attain the single-eyed vision of the Christ mind (Luke 11:34).

**You earlier said that there are two main factors that pull us into the mass consciousness. One is obviously our family, what is the other one?**

The other factor is pressure from those who have set themselves up as being above you, as being a power elite who believe they are entitled to rule the general population. Whereas your peers are afraid that you will leave them behind or rise above them, members of the power elite are afraid that you will rise above their control. They don't want you to rise to the point where you are no longer controlled by their power plays and therefore might even help overthrow their control over the population.

That is precisely why they killed me 2,000 years ago. If you read between the lines, you will see that it was the power elite of the Jewish religion that killed me, and they did so because they considered me a threat to their control over the people. Fortunately, times have become more civilized, and walking the spiritual path is no longer as dangerous. Nevertheless all spiritual seekers need to be aware that there is indeed a power elite in this world, and they will use any means available to them in order to prevent you – and a critical mass of other people – from walking the spiritual path. Unless you understand this fact, you will be easy prey for their control schemes, and you will not be able to understand why you are not making maximum progress on the path.

The immediate goal of the power elite is to pacify people so that no one stands out from the crowd and takes a stand for truth. Yet the real goal is to prevent anyone from reaching the

Christ consciousness by maintaining control over the population. There are three main elements of their strategy:

- **Ignorance.** Their first goal is to prevent people from even knowing about their potential to reach the Christ consciousness and prevent them from finding the systematic path that leads to a higher state of consciousness. Two examples of ways to accomplish this goal are orthodox Christianity, which denies that anyone can follow in my footsteps, and materialistic science, which denies that there is a spiritual side to life.

- **Misdirection.** Over the millennia, representatives of the power elite have spread a number of false ideas that are specifically designed to prevent people from manifesting Christ consciousness. These ideas spring from the duality of the death consciousness, and they have pulled millions of people into spending their lives defending a relative, man-made belief system or idea. Obviously, this takes your attention and energy away from following the path.

- **Intimidation.** There is a definite attempt to intimidate people into not following the spiritual path or not making it all the way to the Christ consciousness.

**Can you describe how people are being intimidated into not following the path?**

There are three main elements of this intimidation, and they are similar to the excuses that I mentioned earlier:

• **You can't do it.** Some lies promote the belief that you simply cannot become the Christ. One example is the orthodox lie that I was the only Son of God and therefore no one can do what I did. Another lie is the idea that only people born in a certain social class can become leaders. There are many variations of the basic lie that it simply isn't possible for you to become the Christ. They are all wrong. No matter what any earthly authority says, God has given each human being the potential to manifest Christ consciousness. That potential is your Christ self, which truly is the open door that no human – or human authority – can shut.

• **You are not allowed to do it**, and you will be punished for trying. Examples are the idea that it is blasphemy to consider doing the works that I did or that you make yourself equal to God by thinking you can know truth on your own. The goal is to make you believe that you will go to hell for blasphemy or that a worldly authority will punish you. Defy all of them, because no earthly authority has the power to keep you out of Heaven.

• **You are not worthy to do it.** Who do you think you are? How could a person of your birth, status in society or accomplishment possibly think you can be the Christ? How could you think you can rise above the mistakes you have made? Only a small elite can achieve any status on earth, and you shouldn't even be trying. You are a sinner, you have this or that fault, you made this or that mistake and so forth. Take note of how they attempted to intimidate me into not fulfilling my mission. Yet I defied all attempts, and by doing so I demonstrated that we can rise above all earthly limitations. The essence of

Christhood is to rise above all limitations in this world and refuse to let them define who you are. You were created as a son or daughter of God, and no power in this world can take that away from you—unless you let them by allowing them to manipulate your free will.

**Many religions define a set of outer rules for how a person should live his or her life, and they seek to use fear to make people follow these outer rules. You seem to have challenged the religious authorities that promoted this fear-based approach to religion. Yet I assume that doesn't mean spiritual seekers can do whatever they want?**

I did challenge those who had set themselves up as the false leaders who promoted a fear-based approach to religion. When people have descended far below the Christ consciousness, and are lost in duality, it might help them to have a fear-based religion that gives them an outer guideline. Yet as you rise in consciousness, you need to leave this fear-based approach behind. You simply cannot successfully walk the spiritual path – at least you cannot pass a certain point on the path – while you are motivated by fear.

If you study my teachings, you will see that I constantly talked about the importance of love. The essence of my message was that as you rise out of the death consciousness, you rise out of approaching life with fear. As you grow toward the Christ consciousness, you begin to respond to life with love. If you study the New Testament, and read between the lines, you will see that what I was really trying to teach people was that the key ingredient on the spiritual path is to learn how to respond to all situations with love.

Although a rigid outer religion might help people in a low level of consciousness, such dogmatic rules have little value for a true spiritual seeker. Once you sincerely start walking the spiritual path, you need to move out of fear so that your actions and non-actions are motivated by love. You do not refrain from doing something because you fear hellfire and brimstone but because you love life, God, yourself and other people so much that you simply would not even consider doing certain things.

What I am talking about here is that all spiritual seekers need to come apart from certain actions that pull them down into the mass consciousness. However, you should not do this out of fear but out of enlightened self-interest. You come apart from the mass consciousness because you realize that it impedes your spiritual growth. Your motivation for coming apart is that you love something more than the temporary advantage or pleasure you gain from participating in a certain activity.

### Can you give us specific examples of what we need to come apart from to achieve maximum growth?

Sure, but let me first say that there are numerous activities on this planet that will slow down your spiritual growth and pull you into the mass consciousness. Many of these activities are quite commonplace, and they have become so integrated in many cultures that billions of people have been brought up to see them as perfectly acceptable, perhaps even necessary, normal or beneficial. They think it is simply a way of life, and they are very reluctant to consider that it might be self-destructive.

I am not going to list every single activity that can hinder your spiritual progress. People on the path need to develop discernment that allows them to intuitively sense what they need to avoid. It is also important to understand that what might be a hindrance to one person might have no effect on another. Once you rise above the fear-based approach to religion, you realize there are few hard-and-fast rules that apply to every human being.

**I think that will be a difficult message for many people to accept, especially for devoutly religious people who have been following certain rules for a lifetime.**

Yes it will, but it is nevertheless the truth. Such people need to ponder the following statement: "For I say unto you, That except your righteousness shall exceed the righteousness of the scribes and Pharisees, ye shall in no case enter into the kingdom of Heaven" (Matthew 5:20). The scribes and the Pharisees followed all of the outer rules to the letter, yet they did so out of fear or pride. They were not willing to step up to a love-based approach to religion, and that is why they could not enter Heaven.

Yet take note that I am not hereby saying that religious people are wrong for abstaining from certain activities. I am only saying that they need to learn how to do this out of love instead of fear. As I have said before, the death consciousness is dominated by relative opposites. This gives rise to two basic responses that both represent unbalanced extremes. One is the fear-based response taken by many devoutly religious people. These people are driven by a fear of punishment, such as burning forever in hell, and they think they will enter Heaven by following outer rules. You will see many people in orthodox Christian churches who take this approach, and the downside is that these people often become very critical and judgmental toward anyone who does not follow their outer standard. That is why I told people to stop judging (Matthew 7:1-2). The reason being that judging others binds you to the death consciousness.

The opposite extreme is the approach that anything goes, that nothing is really wrong and that if something feels good, it is okay to do it. This approach is taken by many of the people who subscribe to scientific materialism and therefore deny the spiritual side of life and the idea that your actions have long-term consequences for your lifestream. Unfortunately, this approach is also taken by many people in the New Age movement, people who have discovered the spiritual path but are distracted from following it because of an attachment to certain activities.

Again, it is helpful with a dose of realism, as expressed in the saying that you can't have your cake and eat it too. There are certain activities that will inevitably generate imperfect energies, and this will slow down or reverse your spiritual progress. The universe is a mirror, and it functions according to the law of action and reaction. It is necessary for all spiritual seekers to look at all aspects of their lives and consider whether they help or hinder their spiritual growth. This evaluation should not be based on fear but on love. I don't want people to abstain from certain activities out of fear of punishment. I want them to do it because they love growth, they love God, so much that they simply will not do anything to slow down their spiritual progress. The difference might seem subtle to some people, but it is all-important to a spiritual seeker.

**What type of activities will slow down our spiritual progress?**

There are several factors to consider when evaluating whether an activity hinders your growth:

• Does the activity produce imperfect, or toxic, energy? If so, this energy will form a dead weight that will slow down your growth. You will eventually have to transform that energy. Obvious examples are activities that generate negative emotions, such as fear, anger or guilt. Also any activity that violates the free will of others. Basically, any activity that results in a reaction that is less than love will generate toxic energy.

• Does the activity spring from or tie you to one of the lies designed to stop your spiritual growth? Obvious examples are the philosophy of materialism, but also many rigid religions that deny your spiritual potential.

• Any activity that violates the Law of Love. If you do something to another that you don't want anyone to do to you, this will slow down your progress.

• The spiritual path is about rising out of ego-centeredness into God-centeredness. Any activity that makes you more self-centered is opposing your growth. There are many such activities that are considered normal and fully acceptable in today's world. Obvious examples are the cults centered around a worship of power, control, success, money or pleasure.

• The physical body is meant to be a servant, a vehicle on your spiritual journey. As a spiritual seeker, you cannot allow bodily desires to pull you away from the path. This does not mean that you have to abstain from all bodily pleasures, such as sex, but it does mean that you need to control these activities instead of letting them run your life. At a certain stage of the path, you may indeed give up these bodily pleasures altogether.

• Anything that weakens or destroys your spiritual defense needs to be avoided. This applies to any form of addictive substance, such as tobacco, alcohol or drugs. When you are under the influence of such substances, your energy field and subconscious mind are wide open to lower energies that you cannot consciously turn away.

The bottom line is that you cannot serve two masters. You cannot pursue worldly activities and live a "normal" life while making maximum progress on the path. You have to choose whom you will serve, and it is necessary for a spiritual seeker to consider the very first of the Ten Commandments, namely: "Thou shalt have no other gods before me" (Exodus 20:3). The mass consciousness has created numerous "gods" that human beings worship before the one true God. Some of these gods are disguised in the form of religious images or doctrines and some have a worldly disguise. As a spiritual seeker, you need to gradually come apart from the consciousness that worships a false god. You need to stop dancing around the golden calf and start climbing the mountain of God.

When you learn to approach the path with love, you will find it easy to discern which activities you need to leave behind, and you will find it easy to simply let them go. People might benefit from pondering the following quote: "When I was a child, I spake as a child, I understood as a child, I thought as a child: but when I became a man, I put away childish things" (1Corinthians 13:11).

When you anchor yourself on the spiritual path, you are no longer a child so you naturally give up childish things. You attain the clear vision that allows you to conquer the negative pull of the mass consciousness through the greater force of charity, which is really love. Love, then, is the real key to spiritual growth. It is love that will empower you to come apart and belong to the separate and chosen people, meaning people who are elect unto God because they have elected to leave behind everything that pulls them away from coming closer to the Christ consciousness and attain union with their spiritual source.

**You have said that we create through the power of our minds. How are we affected by the thoughts, ideas and images that we take into our minds?**

The Bible contains an important saying: "Where there is no vision, the people perish" (Proverbs 29:18). When you realize that the universe is a mirror, you see that it will reflect back to you what you project into it. These projections are sent out through your mind, as explained in my analogy about the film projector. Based on this simple line of reasoning, it should be obvious that the thoughts, beliefs, ideas and images you hold in your mind have a major impact on what you project into the cosmic mirror.

 We will later talk more about the impact of false ideas so I would like to call special attention to the importance of visual images. Consider my statement: "The light of the body is the eye: therefore when thine eye is single, thy whole body also is full of light; but when thine eye is evil, thy body also is full of darkness" (Luke 11:34). We have talked about your personal energy field, and the field has several energy centers, often called chakras. One such center is located at the center of the forehead and is often called the third eye chakra. My statement partially refers to this chakra because when the chakra is pure, you will "see" with the unified vision of the Christ mind instead of seeing through the filter of duality. When your third eye is pure, your four lower bodies will be filled with light, but when the third eye is polluted with disharmonious images, your four lower bodies are filled with darkness.

My beloved Mother had a major impact on the success. of my mission because she held the immaculate vision, the immaculate concept, for me to the very end. You need to hold this vision for yourself. In this computer age, you have the concept: "What you see is what you get," and this applies to the universe. The images you "see" with the mind's eye are projected into the cosmic mirror, and consequently the images in your conscious and subconscious minds will determine what you get back from the universe. It is therefore extremely important to keep your third eye free from imperfect and disharmonious images.

How do you keep your mind pure? The computer age has also given you the following saying: "Garbage in, garbage out!" If you allow disharmonious images into your mind, you will inevitably send imperfect images into the cosmic mirror, and guess what it will reflect back to you. It is therefore essential for all sincere spiritual seekers to keep their minds from taking in imperfect images. In today's world this is quite a challenge because most people are literally surrounded by such images on television, advertising, magazines, billboards and movies.

The forces that seek to control society are quite aware of the power of vision, and they know that people cannot create an ideal society if they cannot envision such a society. They attempt to control society by controlling what kind of images people see. I can tell you that many movies are engineered to project imperfect images into people's minds, images that make it very difficult for people to attain or maintain the single-eyed vision of the Christ mind. This is especially true for horror movies, movies with explicit sex and movies with violence.

Again, it is helpful with a dose of realism. The earth is a treacherous environment, and one aspect is the images to which people are exposed. You need to guard the mind from imperfect and inharmonious images. This also holds true for music. We have talked about the power of using the spoken word to invoke spiritual energy. The other side of the coin is that sound can be a very destructive force when polluted with disharmonious rhythms and words that are programmed into the subconscious mind through the beat of the music. Sincere seekers need to be very discerning concerning the kind of music they take in. Certain types of modern music are so disharmonious that no good can come from allowing it into your energy field. I strongly encourage people to sharpen their intuition and sensitivity so they can realize which images and which types of music are destructive to their progress on the spiritual path.

# 6 | THE FLOW OF LOVE

**I would like to talk more about the idea that love is the key to spiritual progress, including the concept of enlightened self-interest. I think many people find this difficult to understand because they have been brought up with a fear-based approach to religion. I know I struggled for a long time to understand the importance of love so what is the key to even beginning the change of consciousness that you are talking about?**

As I said earlier, I did explain the secret of life in the teachings I gave 2,000 years ago. The teaching that the universe is a mirror has always been there for those who are able and willing to read between the lines. Yet a spiritual teacher never tells people where they need to go without showing them the road that leads them to the goal. I also explained to people how to achieve the goal of a transformation of consciousness. That message is woven through my teachings, and fragments of it can still be found in the official scriptures.

Once again, look at the statement about turning the other cheek and doing unto others what you want them to do unto you. Look at the statements about loving your enemies and doing good to those that hate you (Matthew 5:54). Do you remember the situation where I was challenged by the Pharisees and they asked me what was the most important commandment of the law?

**Yes I do. You said that the most important commandment is to love God with all your heart, soul and mind and to love your neighbor as yourself (Matthew 22:25-40). You also said that upon those two commandments rested the entire law.**

There is a deeper message behind that statement. When you see it in connection with the teaching about the universe being a mirror, you see that what I am really describing here is a very specific approach to life. It is an approach that is radically different from, diametrically opposed to, the approach to life taken by most people. I am sad to say that the vast majority of Christians have not understood the approach to life that I came to demonstrate. This is in large part due to the fact that Christianity became a fear-based religion. Nevertheless, the important point here is to help people see that what I attempted to present 2,000 years ago was the need to adopt a specific approach to life.

The approach to life that I came to present and demonstrate was very simple. It is that no matter what life throws at you, you must always respond with love! Respond to all situations with love!

The deeper meaning of that statement can be understood only when you understand that the universe is a mirror. When you do understand this fact, you realize and accept that if something bad happens to you that event is not simply produced by chance, nor is it caused exclusively by other people, by God's punishment or by the devil. It is an event that is the direct result of your current state of consciousness and your past actions.

At some point in your past, you sent a cause into the universe, and the universe is now reflecting back to you what you sent out. If what you are receiving back is unpleasant, you can be certain that the impulse you sent out was also unpleasant. You were not doing unto others what you wanted the universe to do unto you. You did not send love into the universe. When you receive an unpleasant response from the universe, you know it is a result of the fact that at some point in the past, you sent an impulse into the universe that was dominated by negative feelings, such as fear or anger.

When you accept this fact, you will not get mad at the universe or feel that God has unjustly punished you. Instead, you will realize that you generated the impulse that the universe is now reflecting back to you. You will then be able to reason with yourself, and in doing so, you will discover a very simple fact.

If you are experiencing an unpleasant situation, your first and foremost concern should be to respond to that situation in such a way that you will not make the problem worse. If you run into a concrete wall, you want to prevent your head from hitting the concrete over and over again. Your response should be determined by an enlightened desire to stop the problem so that the unpleasant condition will come to an end and you can experience a better future.

When you accept that the universe is a mirror, you know what to do. If you respond to the unpleasant situation with negative feelings, such as fear, anger or blame, you will simply send out a new impulse dominated by such negative feelings.

You know that, at some point in the future, the universe will reflect back to you what you sent out. You can now reason that the only way to stop the unpleasant situation, and create a better future for yourself, is to take command of your own thoughts and feelings so that you can avoid responding to the unpleasant situation with negative feelings. How can you do this? You need to respond to the situation with love.

If you want to change your outer situation and avoid repeating the same unpleasant circumstances for the rest of your life – and beyond – you need to change your attitude to life, your approach to life, your state of consciousness, so that you can begin to respond to every situation with love.

Every time you respond to a situation with negative feelings, you send a negative impulse into the universe, and the universe will reflect this back to you in the form of another unpleasant situation. Every time you respond to a situation with love, you send an impulse of love into the universe, and the universe will reflect that love back to you in the form of a positive situation.

The simple fact of life is that if you have built a habit of responding to situations in a negative way, you have created a downward spiral. When negative impulses from the past are reflected back to you, you create more negativity, which is eventually reflected back to you, making you even more negative. This is how many people have boxed themselves in, and their negative attitude to life has literally become a self-fulfilling prophecy. Yet the cause of this condition is that the universe will keep reflecting back to you the negative impulses you send out. The universe has no other option. If you sit in front of a mirror, frowning and screaming profanities, the mirror will reflect that mood back to you. It will continue to do so until you change your tune.

The only way to break that downward spiral, and quite frankly most human beings – even humankind as a whole – are currently trapped in a negative approach to life, is to change the way you respond to even the most negative situations. When you learn to respond to all situations with love, you will inevitably create a positive spiral that will lead to a better and brighter future. You will suddenly find that you will attract positive people and positive circumstances. I realize this will not happen instantly, and the reason is that there are certain mechanical aspects of the universe, which we can discuss later.

Yet although I am giving you a simplified version of the secret of life, the basic idea is true and accurate. The universe is a mirror that reflects back to you what you send out. The only way to improve your outer situation is to improve your approach to life so that you can respond to all situations with love. If you love everything that the universe sends to you, the universe will inevitably love you back.

This is not some far-flung utopian, idealistic pipe-dream. It is a reality that is as mechanical as the fact that if you smile at your mirror, the image in the mirror will smile back at you. Stop sitting in front of the cosmic mirror, waiting for the universe to smile at you before you are willing to smile at the world. Take command over your life and determine to respond to life with love. Keep responding with love, and you will inevitably see that the universe will reflect that love back to you.

**The concept that we need to respond to all situations with love is a very beautiful teaching, and I have no doubt that it is very true and very profound, yet it kind of leaves me feeling... well, I don't know quite how to say it...**

I would like to stop you here. Why are you hesitating to ask me this question?

**Well, you just gave me a very profound teaching, and I don't want to offend you by asking a question that might seem rude.**

I thought that was the problem, and I would like to discuss that. Why do you think you, or any other human being, could possibly offend me?

**Well, quite frankly because during my Christian upbringing I was given the distinct impression that it is very easy for us to offend both you and God, and if we do so, it might have unpleasant consequences, such as a drastic increase in body temperature due to hellfire and brimstone.**

I understand, and I know that many other people feel the same way. It is for this reason that I want to discuss the topic. One of the things I would like to get across in this dialogue is that there is a vast difference, in many cases a fundamental difference, between the way God, myself and my teachings have been portrayed by orthodox Christianity and the reality of who God is, who I am and what my true teachings are about.

I hope to help people see that many of their beliefs about God and religion are contradictory and don't make sense when you take a closer look. A perfect example of such an irrational belief is the idea that a spiritual being, such as myself, could possibly be offended by anything in this world. You might remember the situation where I asked my disciples: "But whom say ye that I am?" (Matthew 16:15). I now ask you: "Who do you say that I am, and what do you say that I am?"

**You are Jesus Christ, and you are an ascended being, an ascended master. You reside in a level of higher vibrations that most people call Heaven.**

That is correct, so what you are saying is that I have now ascended from earth and have earned my permanent place here in the spiritual realm. What do you think it takes for a lifestream to go through that process?

**I have always imagined planet earth as a spiritual schoolroom for our lifestreams, as you described earlier. Winning your salvation is like passing the final exam and graduating from that school.**

That is a good answer, but what I want to talk about is the transformation that the lifestream has to go through before it is qualified to permanently enter Heaven. If you take my parable about the wedding feast (Matthew 22:1-14), you will see that it ends with a man who had entered the feast without a wedding garment. He could not remain at the wedding feast but was bound hand and foot and cast into outer darkness.

I am aware that this sounds very brutal, and it has been misinterpreted by many people, including many Christian preachers. Yet the reality of the situation is that the wedding feast can be likened to entry into Heaven. In order to permanently enter Heaven, you need to go through the transformation of consciousness that I am talking about. You need to get yourself into a frame of mind where you can respond to any and all situations with love. In order to get into that frame of mind, you need to leave behind the state of consciousness, the attitude and the approach to life that causes you to respond to situations with anything less than love. This state of consciousness is what I earlier called the death consciousness, and we can talk about it in more detail later. Most human beings on this planet are currently trapped in a state of consciousness that makes it impossible for them to respond to all situations with love. In this computer age, we might compare the subconscious mind to a computer. As we explain in *The Power of Self*, most people have a number of subconscious computer programs that are activated in specific situations. Whenever their expectations about life are not met, a specific computer program is activated, and it takes over their consciousness so that they respond to a given situation in a way that is not loving. This is the true meaning of being bound hand and foot and living in outer darkness. My parable literally describes a state of consciousness in which you feel that you are separated from God and God's kingdom. You are trapped in "outer darkness," meaning that you are outside the kingdom of God, but the darkness exists in your own consciousness.

In order to permanently ascend to Heaven, you must leave behind this death consciousness and all of the subconscious programs that cause you to respond to life as a computer, meaning that you mechanically respond to input instead of acting as the God-free being that you are meant to be. You are letting the subconscious computer take over your reactions instead of consciously choosing to respond with love. Your lifestream is not in control but allows the subconscious mind to run your life.

I have gone through this process of rising above the death consciousness. I have put on the wedding garment of the Christ consciousness and left behind the human garments of the ego. When you leave behind the death consciousness, you leave behind the tendency to take offense. Do you remember the situation where I was tempted by the devil after my time in the wilderness?

## Sure, but I never quite understood what it meant.

That was really a test to see if my lifestream had transcended a sufficient level of the death consciousness to complete my mission. The devil – in reality a representative of the mass consciousness that currently dominates planet earth – was doing anything he could think of to get me to respond from the death consciousness. If he had been successful, it would have shown that I was not ready to complete my mission or ready to permanently enter Heaven.

One might say that life can be seen as a kind of game. There is a force in this world which is constantly trying to trick you into responding to various situations with a reaction that is not based on love. The only way to avoid being pulled into an unloving reaction is to rise above the egoic mind and its subconscious programming. Doing so is the true meaning of my statement: "The Prince of this world comes and has nothing in me" (John 14:30). When you have transcended the death consciousness, the forces of this world will find nothing in you that they can use to tempt or threaten you into responding with anything less than love.

To make a long story short, I hope you can now see that because I am an ascended being, I have permanently transcended the death consciousness and the egoic mind. There is no way I could possibly be offended by anything you could ask me or say to me. The consequence is that I would like you – and everyone else on this planet – to feel completely free to ask me anything you can possibly think of. People should feel free to say anything to me that they feel a need to say. If you do not feel free, you are falling prey to one of the oldest problems on this planet, namely that people project their own state of consciousness, their own world view and their own attitude to life, upon others. This is especially a problem when you project your own state of consciousness, namely the death consciousness, unto a spiritual being or unto God. Because I have transcended that state of consciousness, I cannot and will not fit into the mental boxes – the expectations – created by human beings who are still trapped in duality.

When people project their mental images upon me or God, they are actually violating the first two commandments (Exodus 20:3-4). They are having other gods, namely the mental images they have created, before the true God. Their mental images become graven images that they take unto themselves and worship, instead of worshiping the true God who is beyond any mental images created from the death consciousness.

I have risen above the death consciousness so I cannot be insulted or offended by anything said from that state of mind. I also realize that most people are still trapped in that state of mind, and as a spiritual teacher it is my calling and my great joy to help people rise above that limited state of consciousness. I feel nothing but love and compassion toward the people who are still trapped in duality. I have no problem with people asking me a question that is still influenced by the death consciousness. If you had already risen above that state of mind, you wouldn't need me to show you the way, would you? I want people to feel free to speak their minds and know that I will not be offended. I will always respond to them with love—sometimes it might be tough love, but it will always be a true love for the growth of their lifestreams. Let us now return to your original question.

**My question was why it is so difficult for most of us to respond to all situations with love. I know I have had periods in my life where that would have been**

**a very difficult message to hear and accept, and I foresee that many people will feel the same way. When we go through a very difficult situation, it is almost impossible for us to be loving so being told that we just need to be loving no matter how tough things are, isn't very easy to accept. I mean, most of us simply don't know how to be loving.**

**I think love is one of the most misunderstood concepts on the planet. It is almost like the weather—everyone talks about it but no one knows what to do about it. I think most people would like to follow your advice, but we simply don't know how to be loving. We don't know how to turn on love.**

I understand, and I agree that love is misunderstood. Let me make it clear that I don't expect that people can instantly turn on the flow of love by reading my statements. Learning to respond to life with love – meaning that you rise above the death consciousness – cannot be done in an instant. It will take time, because you must do what Paul said, namely put off the old man – the carnal human – and put on the new man – the Christed human (Ephesians 4:22-24).

This is a process that will take time, and in today's world of instant oatmeal and instant gratification, we run into the problem that many people aren't willing to take the time and make the effort. Yet once you win your salvation, it will last for eternity so isn't it reasonable that it takes time to achieve that goal?

There are many things that people can do to overcome the death consciousness, and we can discuss them later. Learning how to respond to life with love is a straightforward process. While it might take some time to get there, it is very easy to see how to do it. You say that people don't know how to turn on love. Yet in reality, it is easy to understand what it takes to do this. You simply need to stop turning off the flow of love!

**That sounds like one of the baffling statements you made 2,000 years ago. I am sure most people would like to have a more detailed explanation.**

Let me give you an explanation that I simply could not have given people 2,000 years ago because they did not have the knowledge or even the conceptual language that is needed to understand this explanation. The explanation builds on what we have talked about earlier, namely that everything is made from energy.

Scientists currently believe that energy cannot be created or destroyed. This is a truth with modifications, which science will one day discover. Scientists already know that there are immense amounts of energy stored in the atom itself, and they know that by splitting the atom you can release some of this energy. The truth is that the energy is not only stored in the atoms. At the level of subatomic particles, there is a kind of portal through which the high-frequency energy in the spiritual realm can enter the frequency spectrum of the material universe.

The material universe can exist only because there is a never-ending stream of high-frequency spiritual energy that is constantly flowing into this universe. As the energy crosses the threshold between the two worlds, it is lowered in vibration until it vibrates within the frequency spectrum that makes up the material world. I realize that some scientists will dispute what I am saying or call it oversimplified. Nevertheless, it is basically an accurate picture of the process that leads to the creation of the material world. What you need to add to this picture is a new and higher understanding of the mind.

I assume that anyone who is open to reading this book already realizes that there is more to a human being than meets the eye. Your incredibly complex personality is not the product of the physical body. Every human being is a lifestream, and that lifestream is not a physical being. The lifestream is not produced by the body but simply inhabits the body on a temporary basis. One might say that the physical body is like a car and the lifestream is the driver. Although the car can take the driver farther than the driver could walk on his own, the driver is nevertheless perfectly capable of living independently of the car. Most people realize that the lifestream can survive the death of the physical body, and indeed that is why we are talking about the concept of salvation. Everyone knows that the body has a short life span so if the lifestream could not survive the death of the body, how could the lifestream possibly be saved?

The problem I run into in today's world is that most people, especially many Christians, have an incomplete understanding of the lifestream. This is partly due to the fact that the basic teachings that I was able to give 2,000 years ago have been either distorted of removed from orthodox doctrines. However, the real problem is that mainstream Christianity has not recognized the need for progressive revelation. Throughout the centuries, and especially within the last century, I and my colleagues of the ascended masters have given humankind many new teachings on the lifestream and the soul. Unfortunately, mainstream Christians have rejected most of these teachings, and they are often labeled as "New Age," which many Christians consider to be of the devil. Although we can talk more about the soul later, the important point here is that the core of your lower being is a pure self or Conscious You and it is not made from the same type of energy as the physical body. I attempted to explain this 2,000 years ago in the statement that no man can ascend back to Heaven except the man that came down from Heaven (John 3:13). One interpretation of this statement is that the Conscious You is made from the higher energies of the spiritual realm. The Conscious You descends into the material universe and integrates itself with the faculties of the body, but this does not mean that the Conscious You becomes physical or that its vibration is lowered. The Conscious You is still a spiritual being, and it is meant to be *in* this world without being *of* this world.

What most Christians lack is a deeper understanding of where the Conscious You really comes from. What does it truly mean that the Conscious You is created from the higher vibrations of the spiritual realm? What does it mean that the Conscious You is a spiritual being? As explained in greater detail in *The Power of Self*, the Conscious You was not created to exist on its own. When you look at my statement that no man can ascend back to Heaven save him that came down from Heaven, you realize that there must be some kind of conscious being that existed in the spiritual realm before the Conscious You descended into the physical body. That conscious being is what I earlier called the spiritual self or the I AM Presence. This spiritual self is your true identity. It was created by God, and it was created out of the higher energies of the spiritual realm. God made your spiritual self in his own image and likeness (Genesis 1:26).

At some point, this spiritual being, this I AM Presence that you truly are, decided that it wanted to send a part of itself into the material universe. This is how your Conscious You was formed. Your Conscious You is an extension of your I AM Presence, and as such it can never be disconnected from your

Presence. The true relationship between your Conscious You and your I AM Presence can be compared to a planet that is in orbit around the sun. Your I AM Presence is the sun that radiates the spiritual energy that gives life to the Conscious You.

How does this relate to the flow of love? I have said that the material universe is made from energy that vibrates within a certain frequency spectrum. I have said that the spiritual realm is made from energies of higher frequencies. There is a continuum of vibrations ranging from the lower frequencies of the material universe through successively higher frequencies, until you reach the highest possible frequency, which is the light of God. This is the substance that God created when he said: "Let there be light" (Genesis 1:3). The original light that God created is unconditional, divine love. God is truly a God of love, and he created everything that was ever created out of the energy of love. One might say that everything is maintained by a never-ending stream of love that flows from the highest vibration of God's light down through all levels of the world that God has created.

However, this stream of love does not simply operate mechanically. It is directed by self-conscious, intelligent beings that exist at all levels of God's creation. For example, the Bible says that the earth was created by Elohim, which in Hebrew is a plural word. There are a number of intelligent beings in the spiritual realm who allowed God's love to flow through them whereby they created planet earth. Human beings are meant to help co-create this planet. The Conscious You descended into a physical body because it wanted to help create God's kingdom here on earth. A Conscious You can do this by allowing God's love to flow through it from the I AM Presence. The Conscious You then directs that love and uses it to create a thing of beauty in this world. If the Conscious You maintains the flow of love, everything it creates will be harmonious.

The original purpose for your descent to earth was to be a conduit, an open door whereby God's love could flow into this world. The Conscious You is designed to have the love of God flow through it. This is the natural state of the Conscious You.

Unfortunately, most of the lifestreams who embody on earth have descended into a lower state of consciousness. In this state of consciousness they have gradually shut off the flow of love through them. People have set up various conditions in their minds which causes them to say that in such and such a situation, it simply isn't possible, necessary or right to respond with love. They shut off the flow of love and instead respond with negative emotions that misqualify the pure energies of God by lowering their vibration below the frequency of love.

As explained earlier, planet earth has an energy field around it. Human beings have created enormous amounts of misqualified energy, and this is what forms the mass consciousness. There are a number of energy vortexes that can actually overpower people and cause them to lose control of their thoughts and emotions. This has created a downward spiral, and most people are trapped by this downward magnetic pull. This mass consciousness makes it even more difficult for people to respond to situations with love because the energies of that consciousness agitate people's emotional bodies and make them more prone to respond with fear or anger. When we talk about coming apart and being a separate and chosen people, we are actually talking about coming apart from the mass consciousness that pulls you into responding to life with emotions less than love.

The basic idea I want to get across is that the natural state for you is to have an unrestricted flow of God's love streaming through your mind and your feelings. Most people are trapped in a state of consciousness that has caused them to block this natural flow of love. The only possible way to restore the stream of love is that people must engage in a systematic process whereby they resolve and overcome all of the blocks that stop the flow of love through their lower beings. This process of restoring your Conscious You to its original purity, to its innocence, to a state of grace, is the true process of salvation. This is the reason I said that unless you become as little children, you cannot enter the kingdom of Heaven (Matthew 18:3). Many children naturally allow love to flow through them, and they have not yet acquired a set of conditions that cause them to shut off the flow of love. This innocence must be restored before you can return to the original state of purity that will allow you to be saved. By going through this process, you put on the wedding garment that allows you to enter the wedding feast.

The process of returning to your original state of consciousness has been described by virtually every religion found on this planet. It has been explained in many different ways, but if you are willing to read between the lines, you will see that it is the same process. I described that process 2,000 years ago. Unfortunately, most of my explanation was taken out of the scriptures or distorted beyond recognition. One has to be very intuitive in order to discover the true process of salvation in the doctrines and scriptures of mainstream Christianity.

Nevertheless, the essence of the message that I came to demonstrate 2,000 years ago is that all human beings have the potential to win back the original state of consciousness, the innocence and grace that allows the Conscious You to enter the kingdom of Heaven. Do you remember my statement: "The kingdom of God is within you?" (Luke 17:21). What is within you is your mind, your state of consciousness. The kingdom of God truly is a state of consciousness, and I demonstrated that state of consciousness. I came to demonstrate the process that all people have the potential to follow, namely the process of putting on the mind of Christ. Not all of my disciples under-stood this, but several of them did, and one of them was Paul, as evidenced by the statement: "Let this mind be in you, which was also in Christ Jesus" (Philippians 2:5).

**If I understand you correctly, the situation on earth is the following:**

• **Our conscious selves were created to be con-duits for the flow of God's love into this world.**

• **Because we have descended, or fallen, into a lower state of consciousness, we have shut off the flow of love through our minds.**

• **We have created blocks in our subconscious minds, in our psyches, and these blocks stop the flow of love.**

• **This causes us to respond to life with negative emotions, and because the universe is a mirror, it simply reflects back to us what we send out.**

• **This causes us to feel that we are being treated unjustly by fate or by God so we create even more toxic energy, and the result is that we have created a downward spiral that is literally hell on earth.**

• **We are waiting – or perhaps praying – for God to change our outer situation before we are willing to be loving. We refuse to change ourselves, and therefore God can do nothing for us.**

• The only way to break this downward spiral is to reopen the natural flow of love.

• To do that we must respond to life with love so that the universe can reflect this back to us.

• Yet to learn how to respond with love, we must resolve the blocks in our own psyches that have caused us to block the natural flow of love.

• The process of removing these blocks is the true process of salvation that you demonstrated.

• When we successfully complete this process, we will attain the Christ consciousness that you demonstrated, and thereby we can do the works that you did.

**Is that a correct summary?**

That is a clear and concise summary of the basic reality of life on earth and the challenge faced by all human beings.

**I assume some of the blocks that restrict the flow of love are the toxic energies we talked about earlier?**

Correct. The more toxic energy – such as anger – you have stored in your subconscious mind, the more difficult it will be to respond to a situation with love instead of anger. By diminishing the magnetic pull of the toxic energy, you make it much easier to respond to situations with love. Yet, as we talked about earlier, it is not enough to simply use a spiritual technique to transform the toxic energy. You also need to resolve the limitations in your psychology that cause you to create more toxic energy. These limitations are the computer programs that make you think it is necessary, justified or inevitable that you respond with negative emotions.

# 7 | RISE ABOVE YOUR PAST

**When you talked about the universe being a mirror, you said that whatever happens to us is a product of an impulse, or cause, that we sent into the universe in the past. Exactly what does that mean and how far in the past are we talking about?**

I don't expect a lot of orthodox or mainstream Christians to read this book, except to find something that is contrary to doctrine so they can label the book as being false or of the devil. Yet I hope that many of those who have been disappointed by orthodox Christianity, and who have found that orthodox doctrines cannot answer their questions, will be open to this book. I hope these people will be open to the idea that if you cling to orthodox Christian doctrines, you will never be able to fully accept the idea that the universe is a mirror.

The reason is that, according to orthodox doctrine, the soul does not exist prior to the conception of the physical body. This has created huge problems for Christians who are trying to understand and explain one of the undeniable facts of life, namely that many babies are born with diseases or birth defects. Many Christians believe that when bad things happen to them, it must be a punishment for sins they have committed. The concept of sin is a fear-based version of the idea that the universe is a mirror and reflects back to you in the present what you have sent out in the past. Yet when you apply this to a newborn baby, the Christian doctrines simply cannot explain when the baby might have sinned. If the soul of the baby did not exist before the conception of the body when could the soul have sinned?

I realize that some theologians intellectualize about this and say that the soul must have sinned in the womb, but that simply doesn't make sense to most people. As a result, many Christians have been left wondering, and they have received little help from their churches. The problem with mainstream Christianity is that it is so heavily influenced by a fear-based approach to religion. When you take a fear-based approach, you cling to outer doctrines and if a question cannot be explained by doctrine, you are not willing to look beyond doctrine for an answer. Your only options are to deny the question, to explain away the question through some kind of contrived reasoning, or to discourage people from asking the question. That is why so many Christians have been told: "It's a mystery," when they have asked their minister a question that doctrine cannot answer.

One of my main purposes for releasing this book is to show people the advantages of taking a love-based approach to religion. When you take this approach, you will not allow an outer doctrine to prevent you from finding an answer to your questions about life. If the doctrines of a particular religion cannot give you a reasonable answer, you will open your heart and mind to an answer that is beyond doctrine. That is why I said that if you seek, you shall find (Matthew 7:7). Yet the key is to look for answers in the right place, and I described the right place in the saying: "The kingdom of God is within you" (Luke 17:21). You will not find true answers to your questions by looking outside yourself. You will find them only by looking inside yourself and reaching for intuitive insights from your Christ self.

The answer to the mystery of why certain children are born with handicaps or are born into very difficult circumstances, is very simple. The conditions into which a child is born were produced by that lifestream in prior lifetimes. I realize that most Christians have been programmed to deny the reality of reincarnation, but as I explain in great detail in *The Mystical Teachings of Jesus*, reincarnation was indeed a part of my original teachings. The concept of reincarnation was deliberately taken out of Christianity during the fifth century, and this was done for purely political reasons that had no justification in my teachings.

The simple fact is that a human being is an extremely complex entity. In today's age, many people have used various forms of therapy to go deep within their psychology. When you begin to uncover some of the incredible complexity in the human psyche, you quickly see that there is simply no way such complexity could have been produced in just one lifetime. If you are serious about the spiritual path, you must recognize the fact that your lifestream has had more than one lifetime in which it has created its own psychology and sent causes into the universe that are now coming back as mirror images of what was sent out.

The reason this fact is so essential is that discouragement is the sharpest tool in the devil's toolkit. We earlier talked about the need to awaken people to the existence of the spiritual path so they can realize that there is an alternative to the way of life known by most people. When you do awaken to the spiritual path, it is as if you are spiritually reborn, as if an entirely new world of growth opportunities opens to you. I have seen millions of people who were suddenly awakened to the reality of the spiritual path and started walking that path with great enthusiasm and hope. Yet I have also seen many of these people gradually become discouraged by what they considered a lack of immediate or significant results. In some cases, the enthusiasm disappears suddenly, while for others it takes years before they finally give up.

I can tell you that as a spiritual teacher I would love to see every lifestream discover the spiritual path and follow it successfully. I consider it a tragedy that so many people are sleepwalking through life without knowing about the path. Yet I consider it an even greater tragedy that so many of those who discover the path become discouraged and give up because their expectations were not met. This is a situation that all spiritual teachers would love to avoid, and there is only one way for this to happen.

If you are to successfully walk the spiritual path and reach a breakthrough in consciousness, you must take a long-term view of the path. You must recognize that you have grown up in a society that is dominated by technology which promises instant and guaranteed results. The spiritual path is not automatic or mechanical so the results are not guaranteed. On top of that, the spiritual path cannot produce instant results for most people. The reason is very simple, namely that it is an essential part of the spiritual path that you must undo the imperfect causes you have sent into the universe in the past. If you think this can be done in a few weeks or months, or even in a few years, you are setting yourself up for disappointment. You are literally setting yourself up to fail and become discouraged, and unfortunately many people have given up on the path.

The only way to successfully complete the path is to realize that your lifestream has had many lifetimes in which it has created causes that were sent into the universe. As a result, it will take some time to neutralize these causes and rise above the downward pull of your own past. It is absolutely essential that you adopt a long-term approach and realize that it might take years of hard work before you break through to a higher state of consciousness and a better way of life. Yet I can assure you that if you could see your past and see how many lifetimes you have had to create imperfect causes, you would truly realize that it is well worth the effort to spend a few years of hard work in order to rise above the imperfections of the past.

It is absolutely essential that people adopt the attitude that it will take time to achieve a major breakthrough on the path. That is why I said: "In your patience possess ye your souls" (Luke 21:19). You cannot allow the modern culture of instant gratification to cause you to feel that you are entitled to instant results on the spiritual path. You cannot allow the lack of such results to make you discouraged or angry. The only way to avoid this disappointment is to recognize the fact that your lifestream has lived before and has had a very long time to create imperfect causes and a very intricate psychology, both of which can hold back your progress on the path.

You simply need to recognize that walking the spiritual path requires constancy and hard work. Yet you also need to recognize that if you are willing to take the long-term view and make an effort, you *will* see results. Most people will see immediate results when they seriously apply themselves to the spiritual path. The problem is that when you first find the path, you will often ride a wave of enthusiasm that makes you feel like everything is new and exciting. After that wave of enthusiasm begins to wear off, after the honeymoon is over, you are faced with the reality of some hard work. This is precisely the time when most people get discouraged and when many give up. Yet if you will roll up your sleeves and go to work, you will work through the blocks that are preventing your progress. One day you will break through and realize that you have now passed a point of no return and risen to a much higher level on the spiritual path than you ever thought possible.

> **I don't think I heard about the concept of reincarnation until I was in my teens, but when I heard about it, I instantly accepted it as true because it was the only way to explain so many questions I had, including why people are born into different circumstances. I intuitively felt it was the only thing that made sense.**

I would like everyone to use their intuition to get their own inner confirmation of the fact that their lifestreams have lived before. The problem with the orthodox denial of reincarnation is that when people do not have their questions answered, they are left to reason that when children are born into different circumstances, it must be because God wanted to punish one soul and reward another. This will inevitably seem unfair and unjust to most people. Since most Christians have also been indoctrinated with the orthodox concept that God is angry and judgmental, most of them end up feeling resentment or anger toward God.

Because most Christians have been brought up to fear God, they are not willing to recognize their feelings of resentment or anger. They end up stuffing these feelings deep into their subconscious minds, and as modern psychologists have discovered, whatever you stuff into the psyche will inevitably come out again, and it will often come out in unexpected ways. That is why you see so many Christians who become extremely judgmental and intolerant toward anyone who does not believe what they believe or follow the outer rules that they follow.

Consider how often I was challenged and attacked by the orthodox Jews who were extremely judgmental toward me. Why were they so judgmental? They were judgmental because they were angry at God, and since they were not willing to recognize that anger, they could not resolve it. They had stuffed the anger into their subconscious minds and created a false image of God that allowed them to ignore their anger. When someone challenged their image of God, the anger was brought to the surface and directed at that person. There are millions of Christians in today's world who have fallen prey to the exact same mechanism.

Mainstream Christian doctrines have not been able to answer people's questions so they have denied or ignored those questions. They have done this by building a mental image of what a good Christian should believe and how such a person should live. They use that mental image to judge everyone else, and when people do not live up to their outer standard, their unresolved anger against God is taken out in the form of a harsh judgment of other people.

This is a great tragedy because it causes millions of Christians to misqualify the pure energies of God. When you have unresolved anger against God, it simply isn't possible to respond to life with love. As I said earlier, the most important commandments of the law is to love God with all your heart, soul and mind and to love your neighbor as yourself (Matthew 22:37). You simply cannot love God as long as you have unresolved anger or resentment toward God. I can assure you from long experience that very few people are able to resolve their anger against God without recognizing the reality of reincarnation. That is why the concept of reincarnation is essential to anyone walking the spiritual path.

**When I first heard about reincarnation, I heard about the Eastern version, which I found to be too fatalistic. I couldn't accept that everything was determined by karma from past lives and that there was nothing I could do about it. I have since found a more optimistic view of reincarnation, and I wonder if some of the resistance many Westerners feel about reincarnation is that in the West we are not fatalistic but very optimistic. We find it difficult to accept that there could be conditions we cannot change.**

A good observation, and a very true one. It is a great tragedy that orthodox Christianity took out the concept of reincarnation. The main reason is that it prevents people from finding answers to the questions about life. Another reason is that so many people, especially in the present age, are forced to look elsewhere for such answers. Over the past several decades, many Western spiritual seekers have been exposed to the Eastern concepts about reincarnation because there wasn't a well-known Western alternative. Unfortunately, several Eastern cultures have developed what you correctly call a fatalistic view of reincarnation. Some of them believe that your present circumstances are basically set in stone because they are predetermined by your karma from past lives. Because you cannot change your past, you can do nothing to change your present circumstances. Some cultures even believe that if you save another person's life, you interfere with the person's karma, and therefore you become responsible for his life. This is an incorrect view of reincarnation.

Many Christians have a somewhat superficial view of my parents. They think that Joseph was just a simple carpenter and that my mother was an ordinary housewife. Nothing could be farther from the truth. My mother was brought up as a temple virgin and my father was an initiate of a very sophisticated mystical movement that is now unknown. Both of my parents had a deep understanding of the spiritual mysteries of God, and they imparted that understanding to me during my childhood. Both of my parents accepted the reality of reincarnation, and so did I. During my travels in the East, I was exposed to the Eastern concept of reincarnation, and I had much the same reaction to it as the one you described. When I started my mission in Israel, I taught a much more optimistic and, to use a modern word, pro-active version of reincarnation.

The basic idea of reincarnation is that whenever you commit an imperfect act, what Christians call a sin, you create what in the East is called karma. With today's more sophisticated understanding of energy, we can say that whenever you misqualify the energies of God with a fear-based vibration, you send an imperfect energy impulse, an imperfect cause, into the universe. The cosmic mirror will inevitably return the energy to you. However, because it takes time for the energy impulse to come back, it will not always come back to you in the same lifetime in which it was generated.

The conventional concept of reincarnation states that everything that happens to you in your current life is a product of the karma you created in past lives. Many people have come to believe that you cannot change your karma, you cannot change your past, but this is incorrect. Karma is simply an energy impulse that is being reflected back to you by the cosmic mirror. As I explained earlier, you can invoke high-frequency spiritual energy to create a shield around your energy field that protects you from imperfect energies. Likewise, you can invoke high-frequency spiritual energy to consume the imperfect karma from your past before it actually manifests as a negative event in your life. The true concept of reincarnation is that you can indeed change your past because there are several things you can do to neutralize the negative karma before it comes back and disturbs your present circumstances. One of the main messages I want to get across in this book is that no matter what mistakes you have made in the past, no matter what sins you have committed, no matter what karma you have made, you have the potential to rise above it all. You can do that by walking the path to personal Christhood and putting on the mind of Christ. When you follow that path, you rise above all of your sins, and they are washed white as snow (Isaiah 1:18) by the spiritual light you invoke. Thereby, your lifestream will be free from planet earth, and it can ascend to the spiritual realm.

Some Eastern versions of reincarnation teach that as long as you have imperfect karma, your lifestream is not free to ascend to the spiritual realm. It must come back to earth in what is often called the wheel of rebirth. This is a correct idea, but what is not correct is that some Eastern religions portray this as a never-ending process, as a treadmill or merry-go-round. The reality of karma and reincarnation is that you can rise above the wheel of rebirth and be free to permanently ascend to the spiritual realm. This is indeed the path that I came to teach and demonstrate. I taught the true concept of reincarnation to my disciples, but because of the prevalent attitudes of the time, I could not teach it freely to the multitudes. They simply would not have been willing to accept it, and that is why I taught the multitudes in parables but expounded all things to my disciples (Mark 4:34).

**Are you saying that anytime we respond to a situation with anything less than love, we are making negative karma?**

That is correct. If you respond to a situation with anything less than love, you misqualify God's pure energy, and thereby you create a low-frequency energy impulse that is sent into the universe. When that impulse is returned to you by the cosmic mirror, it comes back as what Eastern religions call bad karma.

I know this is a brutal fact that many people will find difficult to accept at first. Incidentally, this is one of the major reasons so many people in the West refuse to accept the reality of reincarnation. Many people realize, at least subconsciously, that they respond to most situations with less than love. If they were to acknowledge that they have had many lifetimes to create negative karma, they would feel overwhelmed and feel as if it was impossible for them to neutralize all the bad karma.

This is based on a psychological mechanism, namely that people will not recognize a danger from which they think they have no defense. Many lifestreams are not willing to admit that they have created negative karma in past lives because they believe there is no way to escape that karma. They believe they have created so much karma that they could not possibly make up for it in this lifetime. It is my hope that this book can help people understand that it is not only possible to neutralize the negative karma from the past but that it is quite easy to do so.

Throughout the ages, we of the ascended masters have given people numerous spiritual techniques for neutralizing bad karma before it manifests as negative events in your life. Baptism, prayer, communion and good works are just some of the ones I gave 2,000 years ago. Today, humankind has risen to a higher level of consciousness, and therefore the ascended masters have been permitted to release much more powerful techniques for neutralizing past karma. As a result, many people could actually neutralize all of their negative karma in this lifetime. This is a major dispensation and an incredible opportunity for all true spiritual seekers. I truly hope this book can inspire people to make use of the tools that are available in this day and age. I can assure you that time has truly been shortened for the elect (Matthew 24:22), meaning that those who elect to use the spiritual tools that have been released in this age can shorten the time it takes for them to balance their karma and win their eternal freedom as immortal spiritual beings who do not have to return to embodiment on earth.

**Can you give a more detailed description of how we make karma? For example, how does karma relate to your teaching about turning the other cheek? Do we make karma when other people do something negative to us? For example, many Christians are afraid that if they are forced to listen to what they call false ideas, they will commit a sin.**

To understand how you make karma, you must begin with the recognition that everything you do is done with God's energy. Human beings use God's energy through their actions, but also through their thoughts and feelings. You are responsible for what you do with God's energy, but you are not responsible for what other people do to you.

Let us imagine a situation where you are exposed to an incorrect idea—incidentally this happens to most people on a daily basis through mainstream media. If you did not deliberately choose to seek out the source of the idea, there is no way you can make karma by listening to the idea. However, you can make karma if you respond to the idea or the situation in a negative way. If you become fearful, irritated or angry, then you will make karma because those feelings will misqualify the energies streaming through your consciousness. Likewise, if you were to accept false ideas and live your life according to them, you would make karma. In short, you cannot make karma for other people's actions. You can make karma for your reaction to other people's actions.

This is one of the major principles behind the Golden Rule, but unfortunately most Christians have not understood the profound truth behind this rule. You live in a world in which every human being has free will. You also live in a world that is very far removed from God's original purity and intent. Many people have descended into a very low state of consciousness in which they are completely self-centered and selfish. When you enter this world, it is inevitable that you will be exposed to people who will treat you in a way that is out of harmony with the laws of God.

When a person mistreats you that person will automatically make karma. There is no way the person could ever escape the responsibility for that karma, although it might not come back to the person in the present lifetime. This is clearly described in the Bible in the saying that a man will reap what he has sown (Galatians 6:7). It is also clearly stated that God will return all karma to a person: "Vengeance is mine; I will repay, saith the Lord" (Romans 12:19).

Because people do not understand this, it often happens that when a person is mistreated by another, he or she either takes negative actions or enters into negative thoughts and feelings concerning the other person. This means that the second person has now made karma in the situation. Instead of a situation where one person violates the laws of God and makes karma, we now have a snowball effect where the second person is tempted into also making karma. This can cause a downward spiral between two people that can continue to escalate for the rest of that lifetime and even over many lifetimes. This is what you see throughout the world, not only between individuals but also between groups of people, such as families, communities, nations, religious groups and races.

Today's world presents an incredibly tangled web of karmic relationships between people. This web is so complex that it presents numerous challenges for evolving lifestreams and for their spiritual teachers. I came to set people free from this web of karmic entanglements, and I clearly realized that in order for people to be free, they had to somehow break the negative spiral of making more and more karma with each other. As the primary tool for breaking this endless cycle of karmic relationships, I gave the Golden Rule.

If someone comes up to you and slaps you across the face that person has made karma. If you hit the person back or become angry or even fearful, you will also make karma. However, if you can remain completely non-attached and turn the other cheek – if you respond to the situation with love – then you will not make karma from the situation. Thereby, you will set yourself free from any karmic spirals, and you can simply move on from the situation without having it slow down your growth.

Unfortunately, because my teachings on karma and reincarnation were removed from Christianity, most modern Christians have not understood the profound principle behind the Golden Rule. They have not fully internalized the Golden Rule, and that is why so many modern Christians find it difficult to follow this rule with the true spirit of non-attachment that comes from unconditional love. Even if someone harms you severely, an understanding of karma will make you realize that the person can never escape responsibility for his or her actions. You have absolutely no reason to seek to punish the person or to entertain negative thoughts or feelings toward the person. You can let go of the situation and lovingly allow God to return the person's karma in due time. This sets you free to move on from the situation instead of entering into a negative spiral that can continue to build over many lifetimes.

Many souls have created such a strong karmic tie to other souls that they feel like they can never get away from these people. The main motivation for following the Golden Rule is really whether you want your personal freedom or whether you want to remain in bondage to people who have harmed you in the past and perhaps are still harming you in the present. The only way to be free of such people is to fully internalize the Golden Rule and turn the other cheek with unconditional love. This love becomes the person's judgment and will ensure the return of the person's karma. It will also set you free to move higher on the spiritual path. For each time you respond to another person with love, you move one step closer to Heaven. You come apart from negative people and become a chosen people (Joshua 24:22) because you have chosen to respond with love.

**That really takes my understanding of the Golden Rule to a whole new, and much more meaningful, level. I wish all Christians – and for that matter all people – could accept this one truth. It could literally change the world.**

I share that desire, yet I also know that a lifestream has to reach a certain level of maturity before it can accept and internalize this truth. Some people are still so burdened by the past that they simply cannot see beyond their anger or desire for revenge over others.

**What does it actually take for a lifestream to rise above its mistakes, its karma, from the past?**

Let me give you a brief overview of the situation faced by most lifestreams. The I AM Presence and the Conscious You of every human being was created in the spiritual realm. After being created, you made the choice that you wanted to experience life in the material universe and you wanted to help co-create God's kingdom on earth. Your I AM Presence created your Conscious You, which then descended into the material universe and took on a physical, or human, body.

When a lifestream descends into the material universe, it becomes subject to the laws used to create the material world, including the Law of Cause and Effect. This law states that a lifestream is responsible for how it uses God's energy. If you use energy in harmony with the laws of God, you generate beneficial, or constructive, energy, which we can call good karma. Such energy will serve to expand and enhance God's creation, and it becomes your treasure laid up in Heaven (Matthew 6:20). Any energy below that frequency will serve to break down and limit creation, including your own creative expression. This is what we can call bad karma.

After lifestreams lost contact with their spiritual selves, they also lost a clear perception of the laws of God. The Fall of Man was a fall in people's consciousness. People simply descended into a lower state of consciousness in which they could no longer maintain contact with the spiritual realm. Because they no longer had this contact, lifestreams inevitably began to misqualify the pure energies of God. The Law of Cause and Effect states that if a lifestream misqualifies God's pure energy, the lifestream is responsible for requalifying the energy by raising the vibration of the energy to its original purity. The lifestream must balance the negative karma before it is free of its past mistakes. When a lifestream misqualifies spiritual energy, it cannot simply leave the earth behind. As long as the misqualified energy remains in the material universe, the lifestream has a debt to life, it has a tie to the material universe. If a lifestream misqualifies energy on earth, it creates a gravitational force that pulls it back to this planet. A lifestream cannot ascend to the spiritual realm until it has paid its debt to life and purified all misqualified energy.

Another consequence of the misqualification of energy is that it causes the physical body to age and break down. That is why the life span declined until it reached its lowest point during the stage of the caveman. For some time, the life span has been increasing, indicating that humankind is in a cycle of growth. People are gradually learning to use God's energy without misqualifying it. Obviously, this learning process is far from complete but it is nevertheless a positive trend.

God never intended for any lifestream to create a debt of misqualified energy, or karma, that would tie it to the material world. God intended a lifestream to descend to earth, live until it had achieved everything it wanted to achieve and then ascend back to the spiritual realm. When some lifestreams misqualified energy, they could no longer ascend. God had to give these lifestreams an opportunity to return to earth and purify the misqualified energy. This became the process of reincarnation. A lifestream must keep reincarnating on earth until it has purified all misqualified energy created here. The lifestream has then paid back its debt to life and can permanently ascend to Heaven.

The consequence of the misqualification of energy is that one of the main requirements for personal salvation is that you purify all misqualified energy that your lifestream has accumulated in the material universe.

**Are you saying that we can and should purify this energy, or balance our karma?**

Certainly. There are many ways to balance karma. To fully understand the process of purifying energy, you need to realize that there are two types of misqualified energy. One might say that there is an internal energy and an external energy. When you commit an act that is not in harmony with the laws of God, two things happen.

One is that the act generates an energy impulse that is sent into the world. Albert Einstein speculated that if you travel away from earth and keep going in the same direction, you will eventually return to your starting point from the opposite direction. The space-time continuum forms a closed loop. When you send an energy impulse into the universe, it will travel through the space-time continuum, which is truly an energy continuum, and it will eventually return to your lifestream. Obviously, this will take some time, and that is why people generally do not receive an immediate return of the negative karma they send out.

The other thing that happens when you violate the laws of God is that you create an amount of misqualified mental and emotional energy. When you respond with less than love, you generate mental and emotional energy that vibrates below the critical level. This energy is not sent into the universe; it is stored in your personal energy field which is part of your soul. Your soul will carry this energy with it even after the physical body dies.

I realize that many people do not want to accept the idea of reincarnation because they do not want to accept personal accountability for what they have done in the past. Nevertheless, the inescapable fact is that most people have reincarnated hundreds of times on this planet. They have had hundreds of lifetimes to generate imperfect causes that were sent into the universe. They have also generated negative mental and emotional energy which has accumulated in their personal energy fields. This karma and toxic energy becomes a burden to the lifestream. It can greatly limit your ability to express your true individuality, to express your God-given creativity and to enjoy life. Consequently, it is in your own best interest to start removing this energy.

If you are serious about spiritual growth, you have to lighten your load of misqualified energy, both the energy stored in your personal energy field and the energy coming back to you from the universe. The expression that a person is between a rock and a hard spot can be applied to what we are talking about. A lifestream is literally caught between the rock of the misqualified energy stored in the soul's energy field and the hard spot of the karma that is being returned by the universe. To achieve maximum spiritual growth, you need to find effective ways to deal with this misqualified energy.

As explained earlier, there is nothing difficult or mystical about purifying misqualified energy. You simply need to raise the frequency of the misqualified energy, and you do that by invoking spiritual light from Above and directing it into the misqualified energy. This is a natural process that any person can learn. I might add that any person who is serious about spiritual growth needs to learn this process.

### Can you give us some practical ways to purify the misqualified energy?

We have already talked about how to purify your energy field so let me focus on how to deal with the returning external energy, returning karma. When you generate a wave of toxic energy that is sent into the universe, it takes some time before the energy comes back to you. It generally takes several lifetimes before the karma comes back. The time it takes for the energy to return is a grace period. You can look at energy as a debt to life. If you use your time wisely, you can become a spiritual millionaire before you have to pay back your debt.

In that case, paying back your debt will not disrupt your life. That is why I told people to lay up treasures in Heaven (Matthew 6:19). When your thoughts, feelings and actions are in harmony with the laws of God, you generate constructive energy which becomes your positive karma, your treasure in Heaven. If you have enough treasure, it can cancel out the returning negative karma.

Almost every religious ritual or practice was designed to help people produce positive energy, positive karma, and thereby pay back their debts to life. You can also do this through your positive thoughts, positive emotions and positive actions. This is what the Bible calls good works. Take note that good works are not confined to certain outer actions. Good works include your thoughts and feelings because an outer action is simply the effect of a psychological cause that starts at the level of thoughts and emotions. A negative act does not appear out of nowhere. It begins in the form of a negative thought which releases a negative emotion that eventually triggers the outer action.

If you take a closer look at the Bible, you will see that the Law of Moses was concerned with reforming people's outer actions. In my Sermon on the Mount I stated that it was not enough to refrain from adultery; you have to overcome the desire for adultery (Matthew 5:28). We have now entered a new spiritual cycle in which people need to realize that it is not enough to refrain from negative acts. You also need to purify your thoughts and feelings.

If you do not create positive karma to cancel out the returning karma, you will inevitably reap the consequences of that karma. This can manifest in the form of accidents, diseases or other negative events in your life. Many people wonder "why bad things happen to good people." Well, the reason is that those good people were not so good in a past life, and they are now reaping what they have sown.

You will inevitably balance the karma you made in past lives, because the cosmic mirror will reflect it back to you. Your choice is how you balance that karma. Do you engage in good works and use spiritual techniques to consume the karma before it manifests as negative events, or do you choose to balance it the hard way? I realize that because my original teachings on karma and reincarnation were taken out of Christianity, most people in the Western world are not aware that they have a choice in the matter. However, they do have the choice to educate themselves by looking at knowledge from non-Christian sources and then make the appropriate changes in their lives.

Another way to balance karma is to use a spiritual technique to invoke high-frequency energy to raise the vibration of the returning karma. The techniques for transforming the toxic energy stored in your energy field will also transmute your returning karma. However, it is essential for all true spiritual seekers to realize that it is not enough to simply transmute the energy, internal or external, that has already been misqualified. You also need to stop creating more of such energy, and the only way to do that is to go into your psychology and remove the wounds and subconscious computer programs that cause you to engage in imperfect thoughts, feelings and actions.

**One last question on karma. You earlier said that whenever something happens to us, it is safe to assume it is a result of something that we did in the past. But you are also saying that we are not responsible for the actions of others. I know many spiritual people who would say that if someone accuses you**

**of something, it must be because you have done the
same to that person in the past. Is that the way it is?**

This is another example of the simplistic view of karma promoted by some Eastern teachings. In reality, things are not
quite as linear. I have said that planet earth is today an incredibly tangled web of karmic connections. I have said that many
people have created negative karmic spirals with each other
and are continually reinforcing those spirals.

Let us talk about people who are still engaged in such
downward spirals and people who have started the spiritual
path. For those who have not yet started the upward path,
their return of karma is very often quite linear in the sense that
what others do to them in this life, they have done to others
(not necessarily the same lifestreams) in a past life. You see
this in many places on earth, but the Middle East is a primary
example of how some groups of people have been fighting
against each other for many lifetimes. One group kills a member of the other group and that group retaliates in kind. As
long as you respond based on "an eye for an eye" you will
reinforce the karmic spiral.

Yet when you start the spiritual path and honestly seek to
change not only your actions but also your state of consciousness, you will rise above the "an eye for an eye" mentality and
start to turn the other cheek. This will cause you to eventually
work through the karma coming from your actions. You then
start on the next level of karma, namely that made from your
reactions to situations. I have said that whenever you respond
to a situation with less than love, you make karma. Say someone accused you in a past life and you responded with great
anger. You did not take action against the other person, but
you did have great anger and this created karma. This karma
might precipitate as a situation where you are accused in this

lifetime. If you again respond with anger, you create more karma, but if you can respond with love, you balance karma.

We can also say that if you responded with anger to a situation in the past, you have an attachment to something on earth. As you reach the higher stages of the path, you need to be tested by being exposed to situations that reveal your attachments. If you can experience such a situation and work through your attachment, you can make a major leap forward on your path. You could theoretically have requalified all energy from a past situation but still be exposed to a situation as a test to see if you have overcome your attachments. Thus, it is wise for spiritual seekers to consider every situation as a test that can help them expose their attachments.

Finally, it should be mentioned that not everything that happens to you in this lifetime is necessarily a result of something you did in a past lifetime. We cannot discount free will and the possibility that people can choose to make new karma for themselves in this lifetime. What other people do to you will not always be related to something you did in the past, it can simply be the result of their choices. People are making ego-based choices all the time.

However, it is still wise to use all situations to look for your personal attachments. The fact is that the Law of Free Will gives people the right to make karma, and you have no need to react to that with anything less than love. It is not the actions of others that will get you to heaven; it is your non-reaction to the actions of others that will get you to heaven.

# 8 | RISE ABOVE YOUR PSYCHOLOGY

**You have talked about the need to resolve blocks in our psychology, but it has been my experience that many people are reluctant to do this. When I grew up, the general attitude was that only people with a severe mental illness would do any kind of work on their psychology. I know this has softened somewhat with the self-help and New Age movements, yet I still find that many people – especially men – are reluctant to look deeply within the psyche. Can you explain why it is beneficial for us to do this?**

I understand that many people have been brought up with the attitude you describe. I agree that this is especially a problem for men who have been brought up with the traditional culture that big boys don't cry and that men are not allowed to show emotions. It can be difficult for such men to engage in psychological healing, which does require you to deal with emotions. Let me give a few thoughts that might help people get over the hump and find ways to overcome their psychological blocks.

Let us begin by stating the fact that many people were brought up to believe that there is nothing you can do to take command over your psychology. It is the product of hereditary and environmental factors, and once you grow up, there is nothing you can do to change who you are. This is an obvious lie promoted by the forces who do not want you to grow spiritually. The very fact that everything is energy, and that you can change the vibration of energy waves, demonstrates that you can change any aspect of your psychology. You are not simply a victim of environmental and hereditary factors. You can take command over your psychology and systematically change the conditions that stand in the way of your peace of mind, happiness and personal Christhood.

Let us be realistic. When you look at the self-help movement, the New Age movement and even much of the revival in more traditional religions, you will see that it is largely driven by women. In today's world, women are clearly playing a more important role than men in terms of driving spiritual growth. One of the main reasons is that women are generally more open to changing themselves by working on their psychology. I would like to see a more balanced situation where men and women participated more equally. Yet for that to happen, more men must step up to the plate and use the tools for psychological healing that are readily available today.

Simply consider what you want: growth or stagnation? I have earlier said that an essential element of spiritual growth is to transform the toxic energy stored in your energy field and the external energy, the karma, that is being returned to you by the universe. You can use a spiritual technique to do this, and many men are open to using such rituals. Yet imagine that you use a technique to transform a certain amount of energy but you immediately create more misqualified energy. You might end up making a valiant effort, yet you either make no progress or do not make the maximum amount of progress.

If you are truly committed to growth, you need to stop misqualifying God's energy, and the only way to do that is to resolve the blocks in your psychology that cause you to create toxic energy and karma. This argument should have a great appeal to men, who are often more analytical. You simply need to make a balance sheet of your income, meaning the amount of toxic energy you transform, and your expenses, meaning the amount of new energy you generate. If your expenses are higher than your income, your progress is negative. Only by minimizing your expenses can you maximize your progress.

When you reach a certain level on the spiritual path, you will naturally attain an uncompromising commitment to your growth. You will begin to feel such a love your I AM Presence that you simply will not let anything prevent you from moving closer to union with it. It becomes a natural part of your path that you take active measures to resolve your psychology. You simply will not let psychological limitations stand in your way.

Today, there are far better tools for healing than what was available 2,000 years ago. If the current tools had been available back then, I would have had all of my disciples use them. My goal was to raise them up to full Christhood. This did not happen, partly because we did not have the best possible tools for psychological healing. Consequently, my disciples did not overcome some of their psychological blocks and it prevented them from exercising their full potential. This partially explains why Christianity did not become the movement I wanted it to be. Today, I am looking for those who are willing to be my disciples in this age, and because the tools are now available, people have a far better opportunity for manifesting their Christhood. I need those who can teach my true teachings today, but to teach my teachings you need to embody them. In order to embody my teachings, you must overcome the psychological blocks that prevent you from accepting your Christhood.

As you grow up, you learn a great number of things about the outside world or even your physical body. Unfortunately, most people grow up in a culture that teaches them very little about the one factor that determines their life experience. Your psyche is the main factor that determines whether you are happy or unhappy. When you know that the universe is a mirror, you see that your happiness does not depend on external factors. It depends primarily on the conditions in your own psyche. If you have psychological blocks and wounds, you will not be happy or have peace of mind as long as those wounds remain unresolved. If you truly want happiness and spiritual growth, wouldn't it be natural to learn how the psyche works and how you can get out of your own way? You have heard the saying: "You are your own worst enemy," and that is perfectly true for a person with unresolved psychological wounds. Yet it is quite possible to heal those wounds. Once again, you can do a balance sheet. Would you rather carry your psychological wounds for the rest of your life and continue to feel as unhappy and unfulfilled as you feel now? Or are you willing to make a concentrated effort to heal your wounds and be free of their influence forever? When you reach a certain point on the path, this becomes an easy choice.

Some people think that because they had an easy childhood, they don't need to work on their psychology. Yet when you realize the reality of reincarnation, you see that even if you had an easy childhood this time around, you probably didn't have it easy in all of your past embodiments. Psychological wounds are wounds of the soul, and they are carried over from lifetime to lifetime. Once again, it is very healthy for spiritual seekers to have a dose of realism and recognize the fact that planet earth is a treacherous environment. Simply take a quick look at history and consider humankind's violent past. It is highly likely that every human being has experienced traumatic situations in past lives, and therefore everyone can benefit from using the right tools to heal such trauma.

**I know that psychology is a very complex topic that we can't cover in depth, but is there some concept that can help people get started on healing their psychological wounds? I mean, what is the least people should know about psychology?**

*First step*

I earlier talked about the two Rs, namely revelation and ritual. I also explained that the first step toward taking command over your psychology is to diminish the gravitational pull of toxic energy. The reason being that as long as your emotional body is in turmoil, you simply cannot dig into your psychology and heal your wounds. All of your energy and attention is spent on dealing with an ongoing crisis that leads from one disaster to the next. The very first step is to get out of this crisis mode, and the best way to do that is through an efficient spiritual ritual. Once again, my suggestion is to use decrees and invocations for protection and transformation.

I know there are many organizations that promote various spiritual techniques as a magic bullet that will solve all of your problems. Yet it simply isn't possible to heal your psychological wounds exclusively through ritual. The reason is that everything is subject to your free will. What causes you to generate toxic energy is that you choose to engage in imperfect thoughts and emotions. This choice usually springs from the fact that you either have an incomplete understanding of life or that you have accepted certain erroneous beliefs. This acceptance of false beliefs likely happened in past lifetimes so these beliefs might have become deeply ingrained in your psyche. Yet the acceptance of erroneous beliefs always begins with a choice. It can be undone by making a better choice.

Let me attempt to give a visual illustration of this. I have said that what keeps a lifestream alive is a constant stream of energy flowing from the spiritual self. You might compare your consciousness to a river. If your thoughts and emotions are pure, the Water of Life can flow freely. You feel a great connection to your spiritual self and you have abundant energy. When you accept an incorrect idea or belief, it is like throwing a rock into the river. If you throw a rock into a stream, you impede the flow of the water. The water has to flow around the rock, and this creates a vortex behind the rock in which debris can accumulate. Once you make the decision to accept an erroneous idea that belief will block the light from your spiritual self. The erroneous belief will misqualify the light, and the misqualified energy will begin to accumulate "downstream" from the erroneous belief. It is like silt accumulating behind the rock in a stream.

Now imagine that a lifestream has had many lifetimes in which it has accepted erroneous beliefs. Each belief is like throwing a rock into the river. Misqualified energy begins to accumulate behind the rock, and it starts filling up the river bed. This will impede the flow of the water and it might dam the stream. When the stream is completely clogged with rocks and silt, people lose all awareness of the spiritual side of life. They forget their spiritual origin and begin to believe that they are material, human beings. Because the conscious mind (and all levels of the soul vehicle) are downstream from the spiritual self, the blocks in the river prevent the conscious mind from seeing the I AM Presence. How can you begin to improve the situation?

RCI

You must start by removing the silt that has accumulated behind the rocks. The silt is misqualified energy. You invoke high-frequency spiritual energy and direct it into the misqualified energy, thereby raising the vibration of the misqualified energy. As you clear away the misqualified energy, you can begin to see the rock, meaning the erroneous belief, that started the process of accumulation. Once you uncover that erroneous belief, you have to undo the original decision that caused you to accept that belief. This must be a conscious process because you have to make a new decision to replace the original decision. This process is described in greater detail in *The Power of Self*.

One might say that the process of spiritual growth is a process whereby you gradually clear the stream of life. You remove the accumulated silt that covers the rocks, and then you remove the rocks from the stream. When you have removed one rock, and all the silt accumulated behind it, you have taken a very significant step forward on your personal path.

In today's age, too many people have grown impatient. Technology and the general consumer culture has given people the impression that they are entitled to instant gratification. Many people think spiritual progress should happen instantly. This is the dream of an automatic salvation, and it is a false dream. If you take an objective look at the situation, you will see that you might have spent many lifetimes throwing rocks into the stream of life. You might have a lot of silt and a great number of rocks that you need to clear before the energies from your spiritual self can flow freely. This process simply cannot be completed overnight.

For many people the process cannot even be completed in one lifetime. However, this should not be a cause for discouragement. If you give up beforehand, you have not even begun the process. Another factor is that God is merciful. God do⁻

not want lifestreams to remain stuck in the material universe, and therefore God has provided numerous ways whereby people can speed up the process of clearing their personal energy fields and their subconscious minds.

### What practical measures can people take to resolve their psychological problems?

Let us begin with ritual. Mother Mary's many invocations are designed specifically to transmute imperfect energy, but they also have the function of making the person aware of the imperfect beliefs that must be overcome. By meditating on and internalizing the words in the invocations, people can make significant progress. I especially recommend the *Song of Life* teachings and invocations [See the website *www.morepublish. com*]. Obviously, spiritual protection is also important so that you don't take on psychological problems from outside yourself.

Yet is it extremely important that people adopt the attitude that they can resolve their psychology only through a greater awareness that empowers them to replace imperfect choices from the past with better choices in the here and now. This should lead to a state of self-observation in which people are always looking for a deeper understanding of psychology in general and a greater awareness of their own psychological blocks in particular.

This greater understanding can obviously be enhanced by reading books or taking classes on psychological issues. Yet it can also be highly beneficial to engage in some form of indi-
~roup therapy that helps you see what you cannot see
isely because an incorrect belief might have been
being for lifetimes, it can be difficult for you to
oing on. Yet it might be relatively easy for other

people to see this, since it is always easier for people to see the splinter in another's eye than to see the mote in their own eye (Matthew 7:3). If you are a serious spiritual seeker, you can benefit from asking other people, either friends or a trained professional, to expose the hang-ups that you cannot see. You can also gain valuable insights by using your intuitive faculties to gain a deeper awareness of what is going on below the level of your conscious awareness.

**Many people are engaged in self-help or empowerment techniques because they want to overcome negative habits. Yet I sense that some people only want to change their actions without going into the deeper causes of a habit. What is your take on that?**

Your observation is correct, but I hope it won't have much bearing on people reading this book. The readers of this book should have passed the point of wanting quick outer results. The key to walking the spiritual path is that you are not simply looking for a quick-fix but that you are looking to create permanent change in your life. You are not looking for short-term relief from a particular problem; you are looking for permanent change that will have a positive effect on your future. To create this permanent effect, it can be helpful to understand more about the layers of the psyche and how actions originate at deeper levels of the psyche.

In modern times, people often look back at the knowledge of previous ages and consider it primitive. Yet in many cases, the ancients had valid wisdom that has been ignored by modern science or orthodox religion. During the Middle Ages, there was a movement that is commonly referred to as the alchemists. I admit that there were many charlatans in the field, and therefore it is understandable that alchemists have a

tainted reputation. However, the reality of the matter is that
the true alchemists represented a spiritual movement. The real
goal of the alchemists was not the transformation of base met-
als into gold. They sought the transformation of the base metal
of the death consciousness, the human ego, into the gold of
the Christ consciousness. The philosopher's stone sought by
the alchemists was the Christ consciousness. The alchemists
had a world view which incorporated the existence of five elements, namely ether, fire, air, water and earth.

The truth is that ether represents the spiritual realm. The
other four elements represent four different vibratory levels,
four aspects, of the material universe. I have said many times
that matter is made from energy that vibrates within a certain
frequency spectrum, and the alchemists called it earth. Right
above that spectrum, you find another spectrum of frequencies. These frequencies are what the alchemists called water,
and they represent emotional energy. Above that is another
spectrum, called air, which is mental or thought energy. Above
that is another spectrum, namely fire, which is also called etheric energy.

There is much to be said about this topic, but my intent is
to give a concentrated teaching on how energy flows through
the human psyche. The psyche can also be divided into four
levels that correspond to the elements of fire, air, water and
earth. The stream of spiritual energy (ether) that comes from
the I AM Presence first enters the etheric, memory or identity body. At this level, the lifestream's sense of identity is
anchored. The energy first passes through the sense of identity, and thereby the energy is colored by the image of how the
person sees itself, God and the world.

After that, the energy passes through the mental body,
and it takes the form of thoughts. A person's thoughts will be
a reflection of the person's sense of identity. Your thoughts

literally spring from your sense of identity, yet your mental body also contains images of how you think the world works. At the next level, the energy passes through the emotional body. When the energy reaches the emotional body, it is already colored by what has taken place in the mental body and the memory body. Your identity body contains your attitudes and basic approach to life. Your thoughts are the products of your sense of identity and your emotions are the products of your thoughts. The energy finally enters the physical, or material, quadrant in which it is translated into actions. Your actions spring from your feelings, your feelings spring from your thoughts and your thoughts spring from your sense of identity.

If you identify yourself as a mortal human being who is a miserable sinner, your thoughts will tend to focus on the negative aspects of life. You will tend to look at life as a threat, thinking that everything you do is likely to make you feel guilty. Your emotions will tend to center around fear and guilt because you constantly expect to encounter situations that will make you feel guilty. You will often seek to do things that will deflect guilt or blame away from yourself, and this puts you in a passive mode that prevents you from enjoying life. Because the universe is a mirror, it will reflect back to you events that seem to confirm your basic view of yourself and life. You will feel trapped on a merry-go-round from which there is seemingly no escape.

Once you understand the correct flow of energy, you can see how to change your actions, your feelings and your thoughts. For ages, human beings have attempted to gain control over their actions. Unfortunately, much of what has been developed in the field of psychology and self-help deals only with the effects and not with the cause. You cannot effectively change your actions without going all the way back to your sense of identity.

If you truly want change, you must take a vertical instead of a horizontal approach. To change your actions, you have to change your emotions and your attitude to life. If you want to change your emotions, you have to change your thoughts and your understanding of how life works. If you want to change your thoughts, you have to change your sense of identity. If you attempt to change your emotions by controlling emotional energy, you will either fail or face an uphill battle. That is why so many people have attempted to use self-help techniques or therapy only to find that they snap back into old patterns of thoughts, feelings and actions.

As you walk the spiritual path and attain personal Christhood, you will begin to uncover and build a new sense of identity as a spiritual being. You will begin to narrow the gap between who you are and who you see yourself as being. The moment your sense of identity begins to change, at that moment your thoughts will also begin to change. Thereby, your emotions and your actions will naturally fall into place.

**As an example of how to overcome psychological blocks, I would like to focus on anger. You have said that many Christians feel a subconscious anger against God that they cannot resolve because they don't accept reincarnation. Many modern healing techniques encourage people to get in touch with their anger. Yet most religious people have been brought up to stuff their anger so they are often reluctant to express it or even acknowledge it. Can you help us understand how to deal with anger?**

I understand why many religious people are confused about anger. It is correct when many modern healing techniques encourage people to go inside and get in touch with the anger that has been suppressed. However, it is important to keep in mind that the purpose for doing this should never be to get people to take their anger out on others. It is not the purpose of these forms of therapy to get you to fly into a rage and beat up on the first person that comes around. The purpose is to help you get in touch with the suppressed feelings so that you can recognize them and thereby resolve them in a constructive manner. There is an obvious difference between letting someone know you are angry at his or her actions and taking your anger out on that person.

Feelings, or emotions, can be described as energy in motion, and they are generated in the emotional body. The emotional body is meant to take the thoughts that are formulated in your mental body and give them movement so that they can manifest in the material realm. Your emotions are meant to flow, and if you attempt to suppress your emotions, you will block the natural flow of energy through your consciousness. This will inevitably cause various psychological problems, and it is highly beneficial for people to use healing techniques to resolve these blocks so that the energy of their emotions can again start flowing naturally. If your emotions cannot flow freely, how can love flow through your being?

The problem with emotions is that they simply give movement to anything that enters the emotional body from the mental body. The emotional body does not discriminate and discern whether something is good or bad, right or wrong, constructive or self-destructive. The emotions simply act on whatever comes into the emotional body from the mental body—or from an outside source.

Yet before you actually allow an emotion to be turned into an action, there is a split second in which you make a decision to act upon the emotion. At that moment, you have the opportunity to override your emotional body and prevent yourself from expressing negative emotions. Most people are not consciously aware of this moment of decision, yet it is always there. The key to gaining self-control is to become consciously aware of the moment of decision so that you can use your conscious mind to exercise control over your emotions.

There are some situations where expressing anger would lead to negative consequences, and therefore suppressing that anger is the lesser evil. The problem appears when people constantly suppress the anger instead of seeking to resolve the cause of the anger in the mental body and even in your etheric body.

The simple fact is that while anger is an emotion, anger does not originate in the emotional body. It comes from a certain attitude to life in the identity body, often a sense of being powerless to change your life. This gives rise to thoughts in the mental body, especially thoughts that cause you to think that life should be a certain way and that if your outer situation does not live up to your expectations, there is something wrong. This can make you think that if the world does not treat you the way you want to be treated, an injustice has been committed and someone must be to blame. This might cause the thought that another person is to blame, and this releases the emotion of anger which can cause you to seek revenge or attempt to punish the other person.

The problem is that most people do not understand how their emotions originate from higher levels. They have not learned to reach up into the mental body and discover the process whereby thoughts are formed. They have not made the effort to examine their basic beliefs and attitudes toward life and see how those attitudes give rise to specific thoughts that then release certain emotions, such as anger. Most people do not have an understanding of what goes on at the subconscious levels of their minds, and both the emotional body and the mental body are below the level of what is conscious awareness for most people. What happens to most people is that when they experience a situation that violates their expectations, they do not see the thoughts that trigger the emotions. They simply experience that their emotional body starts going wild and they feel anger.

At that moment, the anger has already been produced, the fire has already taken hold and you are left trying to put it out. Your conscious mind now has to make the choice as to what it will do with that anger. Some people do not have enough self-control to avoid acting out their anger so they express it in various ways. This often causes a negative reaction from other people, which is reflected back to you. This can lead to the creation of a negative spiral that produces more and more anger. As the emotional energy continues to build, a vortex of energy is formed in your energy field, in your emotional body. This vortex can eventually become so strong that it overpowers your attempts to control it, and you have then lost control of yourself. This is what causes some people to develop a chronic anger that they cannot stop.

Other people, often guided by religious attitudes or doctrines, adopt the belief that feeling or expressing anger is always wrong. They use all of their willpower in an attempt to suppress the anger. Some people are successful in doing this for a time, but again a vortex of energy will start forming in the subconscious mind, and eventually it can become so strong that it overpowers people's conscious willpower. Other people have such strong self-control that they can suppress the anger for an entire lifetime, yet doing so will have various effects on the psyche and the body. Many diseases are simply the physical effects of suppressed emotions, including anger. The approach taken by many Christians, namely to suppress all anger, is not the most healthy approach.

There are two things you can do to develop a more constructive approach to anger. The first one is to use various modern healing techniques to uncover suppressed anger and resolve the cause of those feelings. This means expressing your anger in a way that does not create a negative spiral between you and other people. It is not healthy to take your anger out on other people, although it is healthy to express it in a more controlled environment. Certain modern healing techniques, including gestalt therapy, can help people get in touch with their anger and express it in a way that helps them reestablish the natural flow of energy through their emotional bodies.

The problem with such healing techniques is that even though expressing your anger is helpful in terms of reestablishing the proper flow of energy, the anger you express still represents a certain amount of misqualified energy. It is precisely this misqualified energy that accumulates in your energy field and creates a negative vortex that acts as a block to the natural flow of energy. Unlocking that block through therapy is beneficial, yet expressing your anger does not transform the toxic energy. It would be extremely beneficial for people, and for humanity as a whole – even the planet as a whole – if all modern therapists – and their clients – would become aware of the need to transform the toxic energy.

This is precisely why we of the ascended masters have released techniques for transforming toxic energy, including the decrees and invocations. I would therefore strongly recommend that people combine therapy with the use of techniques for transforming toxic energy. This would greatly speed up the process of healing and lead to much better results.

Now for the second step in the healing process. As I said, your emotions come from thoughts. If you truly want to heal your psyche, it is not enough to get in touch with your anger, to express that anger and to transmute the toxic energy produced by the anger. After you work through the stored anger and reestablish a proper flow of energy through your emotional body, you need to go to the next level, which is to go into the mental body and uncover the thoughts and beliefs that lead to anger. You then need to realize that these thoughts spring from certain decisions you made about how you see yourself, how you see God and how you see your relationship to God. When you uncover this sense of identity, you can then begin to replace the dysfunctional decisions with better decisions.

What I am talking about here is a process of taking command over every part of your being, including your mental body and your sense of identity. This process is the path to personal Christhood, and as you walk that path, you will gradually replace all limiting attitudes and beliefs with higher beliefs. At the end of this process, you will be in complete command of yourself, and you can then respond to whatever happens in this world without having that response dictated by blocks in your emotional body, dysfunctional thoughts in your mental body or even a limited sense of identity in your etheric body. When the prince of this world comes and has nothing in you (John 14:30) whereby he can manipulate or control you, you will be able to respond with love to every situation. This is the true definition of spiritual mastery.

When you have achieved this inner freedom, you will never feel the human anger that most people experience. This form of anger is always based on a sense of injustice and a sense of blame. Someone has done something wrong, they deserve to be blamed for doing it, and you are going to let them know in no uncertain terms. This form of anger always springs from a desire to punish someone, either through physical actions or by making them feel bad about what they did to you. This can include punishing yourself and making yourself feel bad for mistakes you supposedly made. Incidentally, anger that is not directed at another person (for example out of fear) will end up being directed at yourself. That is why many people who were abused as children feel an often hidden anger against themselves, and they need to make an effort to forgive themselves and transmute the anger.

When you rise above this human anger, you will not necessarily always go around being completely soft-spoken in every situation. There are so many things that happen on this planet that are clearly out of alignment with God's law of unconditional love. It is quite appropriate to challenge the wrongdoings of other people, and this might include expressing strong feelings that most people would see as anger. However, as you begin to reach a certain level of Christhood, you can speak sternly and directly without falling into the lower vibration of human anger. You are not expressing feelings in order to blame someone. You are expressing strong feelings in order to shock people out of their current state of consciousness so they might see that what they are doing is out of alignment with the laws of God and therefore can only lead to negative consequences for themselves.

I am aware that as long as people are still trapped in the lower vibrations of the death consciousness, they will not be able to understand this distinction. Yet there is a very clear difference in vibration between human anger and what we might call holy wrath. How do you tell the difference between holy wrath and human anger? Holy wrath can be powerful, but it will instantly disappear once it has accomplished its purpose, and it will not permanently affect your view of or feelings toward another person. Anger will linger with you for a time after it has been expressed, like a smoldering fire that takes a long time to burn out. It can color your thoughts and feelings about another person for a lifetime, or at least until you fully forgive that person.

Holy wrath is an expression of the unconditional love of God, which is not the soft, mushy love that most people know. Unconditional love will not let you stand still in a limited sense of identity. If you insist on holding on to such limitations, a person who has reached a certain degree of Christhood can become an open door through which unconditional love is expressed and challenges your current beliefs. This unconditional love can be expressed in a very stern way in order to shock you out of your current state of consciousness, a state of consciousness that will eventually lead to your own destruction. Obviously, unconditional love does not want you to destroy yourself, and therefore it is willing to be very direct in letting you know that you are on the wrong side of the laws of God.

I did personally become an instrument for this unconditional love of God on several occasions that are recorded in the scriptures. These instances have often been misinterpreted as human anger, and over the centuries many people have used this as an excuse for expressing their own human anger. This is unfortunate because it prevents people from resolving the cause of their human anger and thereby rising to a higher level of consciousness.

I will admit that I did on occasion express human anger, and one example is when I cursed the fig tree (Matthew 21:19). Contrary to the idolatrous beliefs held by so many Christians, I was not the perfect human being, and I had not completely resolved every aspect of my psychology before my crucifixion. I would have reached that point if I had been given a little more time, but as events unfolded, I did not quite resolve every aspect of my psychological wounds and blocks before the crucifixion.

Let me make it clear that anger is not hard-wired into the spiritual part of people's beings, the Conscious You. It is only hard-wired into the human ego. The key to overcoming human anger is to rise above the dualistic state of consciousness that makes you see yourself as separated from your source and therefore separated from other people. When you rise above dualism, you begin to see the fundamental oneness of all life. When you see that you are an offspring of God, how can you be angry with yourself or with God? When you see that other people are offsprings of the same God, how can you be angry with them?

# 9 | ESCAPING THE PRINCE OF THIS WORLD

**You have said that planet earth is a schoolroom for our lifestreams and that every situation is an opportunity to learn. Yet there are some very negative things happening on this planet, and I find it difficult to believe that they were designed by God as an education for our lifestreams?**

The universe is a mirror so it reflects back to planet earth what human beings have been sending out for a very long time. The negative conditions on this planet were not designed by God. Yet one might say that the negative conditions on this planet can serve to teach people the lesson that they will reap what they have sown.

There is a subtle and important distinction concerning evil. Some people, even some religions, have developed the idea that evil is somehow part of God's plan. They think good is only good when it is seen in contrast to evil and that people only grow by dealing with evil. Some people seem to think that the devil is a servant of God and is simply getting the flak for doing what he is supposed to do. These ideas are all incorrect. Evil was not created by God and is not a part of God's plan. It is perfectly possible for lifestreams to grow without ever encountering evil. This is indeed what happened on planet earth until the Fall. It was only by falling into a lower state of consciousness that human beings opened the door and allowed evil forces to enter this world.

Evil forces do not have the function or the goal of setting people free. They have an insatiable drive to enslave people and to keep their lifestreams enslaved forever. These forces want to prove God wrong and they want to steal your spiritual light. This is their entire modus operandi, and there is absolutely no reason for human beings to feel any kind of sympathy for the devil. The devil made his own choices, and he is reaping the consequences of those choices.

While evil is not a necessary part of God's plan, in the here and now evil is a part of life on planet earth. Although this was not part of God's design, it is better to acknowledge the situation and use it to enhance your spiritual growth. Evil can indeed be used to learn certain lessons, but do not fall into the trap of thinking that this somehow justifies or necessitates the existence of evil.

Learn from my example and the example set by the Buddha. When dealing with dark forces, the most important thing to keep in mind is to remain non-attached and turn the other cheek. One of the main goals of dark forces is to steal your energy. They do so by causing people to engage in conflicts. When you fight evil, you inevitably give energy to evil. When you remain non-attached and turn the other cheek, you do not feed evil. You become one with the cosmic mirror, and you reflect dark energies back upon their originators. This is the correct way to deal with evil forces.

**I can attest to the importance of recognizing the existence of dark forces. I have always been very sensitive to psychic energy, and before I learned how to protect myself, it would burden me greatly. Yet I have found that many people are uncomfortable with this topic because science has told them that the existence of demons is old-fashioned superstition. Quite frankly, I don't think modern Christianity has done much to help people understand this topic. I mean, all Christians know that you cast out evil spirits, but most of them tend to ignore the topic because they cannot understand it. Why are so many people reluctant to even consider the existence of dark forces and evil spirits?**

The explanation is simple. The human psyche has a built-in tendency to ignore dangers from which there seems to be no defense. You know that animals have what is called the fight-or-flight response. When confronted with a dangerous situation, the first impulse is to run away. If that is not possible, most animals will defend themselves by fighting the attacker. Yet in some cases, an animal will neither flee nor defend itself. For example, if you scare an ostrich, it will sometimes hide its head in the sand.

What most people fail to recognize is that this response is also programmed into the human psyche. If you tell a person about a danger from which he believes there is no escape or defense, he will refuse to acknowledge the reality of that danger. He might deny that the danger exists or seek to explain it away so that he can ignore it. Or he might turn around and actually attack you for talking about the topic. In today's world, many people have accepted the claims of scientific materialism and the basic belief that if something cannot be measured by scientific instruments, it doesn't exist. Since no scientific instrument can measure evil spirits, such spirits cannot be real but must be the product of an overactive imagination. In reality, some instruments can measure the presence of evil spirits, but this is not yet understood by mainstream science.

As you point out, most Christians also tend to ignore this topic, and the reason is that orthodox Christianity can give no effective methods for protecting yourself against evil spirits. Yet such measures do exist and are available to anyone who is open to following the spiritual path. One obvious example is the decrees to Archangel Michael.

**I can witness to the efficiency of such techniques. Since I was a child, I have been very sensitive to both spiritual beings and dark spirits. I intuitively sensed the existence of evil spirits and how they attacked me. Yet I have to say that before I learned that there was a way to defend myself against such spirits, I was reluctant to consciously acknowledge their existence, and the reason was that, as you explain, I simply couldn't bear to accept a danger from which there seemed to be no defense.**

**It was an incredible relief for me to learn more about evil spirits and thereby learn how I could defend myself. After I started applying techniques for spiritual protection, I truly felt I gained greater control of my life and greater peace of mind. I really believe that such techniques could work for other people as well.**

You are quite right. The simplest way to protect yourself from dark spirits is to invoke the spiritual protection that also seals you from imperfect psychic energies. In a sense one might say that an evil spirit is simply a concentration of imperfect psychic energy. When you invoke a wall of high-frequency spiritual energy around your energy field, it becomes far more difficult for evil spirits to enter your energy field or to project thoughts into your mind.

### Can you tell us how dark forces influence us?

As I said earlier, every human being has learned to protect the body from harmful bacteria. I consider it equally essential for people on the spiritual path to learn how to protect themselves from the influence of dark forces. To successfully walk the spiritual path, you need to be aware that dark forces exist and you need to understand that they are constantly trying to manipulate you and prevent you from making progress on the path. When you understand the methods used by dark forces, it will become relatively easy to protect yourself from their influence. This will greatly increase the speed with which you progress on the path.

It is extremely helpful for people to understand the two main goals of dark forces. The existence of dark forces started when certain beings rebelled against God's purpose for creation. As I explain in *The Mystical Teachings of Jesus* this happened in a precious sphere as that sphere was in the process of ascending. These beings believed it was a mistake by God to give human beings free will because it would lead souls to destroy themselves and become lost. As a result of their rebellion against God's purpose, these beings could not ascend with their sphere. They "fell" into the next unascended sphere and some have continued falling and are now in the material universe. Some of these beings actually took embodiment on planet earth. Other rebellious beings did not take physical embodiment but exist in the energy field that surrounds planet earth. Many of them reside in the emotional body, and from this position they are able to influence human beings.

When a lifestream descends into a lower state of consciousness, it loses its conscious contact with the I AM Presence. Thereby, the stream of spiritual energy that flows from the spiritual self into the lower being will be gradually reduced, and it can eventually be cut off completely. When a being has become cut off from its I AM Presence, it can no longer absorb the energy from the Presence. The vibration of the being's consciousness has become so low that it cannot absorb the high-frequency spiritual energy. In order to survive, such a being must steal energy from its surroundings. It must get energy horizontally instead of vertically.

One might say that dark spirits are no longer able to absorb the vibration of love. However, they can still absorb the frequencies that are generated through lower emotions, such as anger or hatred. Because they cannot receive energy from Above, they cannot misqualify spiritual energy but must steal energy from their surroundings. In order to survive, dark forces must seek to manipulate human beings, who are still receiving energy from the spiritual realm, into lowering the vibration of that energy to a frequency they can absorb. The dark forces seek to manipulate people into engaging in imperfect thoughts, feelings and actions whereby people misqualify God's energy so that the dark forces can steal it and use it for their survival.

When you understand this dynamic, you see that the dark forces on this planet have two main goals. One goal is to prove that God was wrong by giving human beings free will. These beings are completely trapped in the consciousness of pride, and they are not willing to accept that they were wrong from the very beginning. Their life is based on a lie, and that is why I said that the devil was the father of lies (John 8:44), meaning that his rebellion against God was based on a lie. Ever since the rebellious beings descended to this world, they have been trying to prove that they were right by seeking to manipulate people into misusing their free will and destroying themselves. If these dark beings can manipulate people into creating a downward spiral that eventually leads to the destruction of human society or to the loss of individual souls, they will feel that they have proven their point that God was wrong.

②  The other part of their agenda is that by causing people to misuse their free will, people will misqualify the energies of God so that the dark forces can steal them and use them to survive or even to strengthen their power over human beings. As we explain in *Healing Mother Earth*, human beings have misqualified so much psychic energy that there are a number of vortexes in the energy field of the planet. If these vortexes were to continue to grow, they could eventually become so strong that they would overpower the conscious minds of all human beings so they would no longer be able to respond to life with love. Humankind as a whole could then be trapped in a downward spiral that would quickly lead to their own destruction. This is truly the plan of the dark forces, and when you realize their purpose and methods, you see that it is essential for people walking the spiritual path to free themselves from the negative influence of these dark forces.

How do dark forces seek to manipulate human beings? One way is that they seek to project thoughts into your mind. When you realize that everything is energy, you realize that thoughts are simply forms of energy. After Einstein's discoveries, it became easier for people to see that telepathy is a distinct possibility. Every thought generates energy waves, and some of them are sent into the universe. As these waves enter the energy fields of other people, they can potentially influence people's thoughts.

The dark forces have developed quite an ability to project thoughts into people's minds, and I think most people who are intuitive realize that they sometimes have a thought which they can identify as not being their own. The logical conclusion is that the thought was projected into their minds from some external source, and that source could very well have been dark spirits who are always seeking to deceive people.

The main goal for projecting thoughts into people's minds is that the dark forces know that the truth will make you free so they are trying to prevent people from discovering the truth. They are doing this by projecting a number of very subtle and very clever lies into the minds of human beings. Another goal is to project thoughts that will cause people to adopt a negative or self-destructive attitude to life. As mentioned earlier, discouragement is the sharpest tool in the devil's toolkit. A negative attitude will make people more prone to engage in negative emotions whereby they will misqualify the energies of God. To achieve this goal, the dark forces also project waves of emotional energy into people's energy fields. Their goal is to agitate your energy field until you can no longer maintain your peace and harmony. This is what many people call stress, and most people realize that the more stress you have, the more difficult it becomes for you to respond to situations with love.

**It was very profound for me to gain a better understanding of dark spirits because I suddenly began to realize why some people commit such atrocious acts. I grew up in Denmark, and from childhood I was taught about the Holocaust and the atrocious acts committed by the Nazis. I never fully understood how people could be so insensitive to life. Yet it makes sense to me that such atrocities happen**

**because people are manipulated by dark spirits. Is that a correct view?**

It is, insofar as we are talking about human souls. As I said earlier, certain spiritual beings fell from Heaven and ended up on planet earth. Some of these beings are trapped in the consciousness of pride and are not willing to admit that they could possibly do anything wrong. If you are not willing to admit your mistakes, you cannot correct those mistakes. There is no limit to how far such a being can move into the consciousness of evil, the consciousness of death, the consciousness of hell. Human beings were not created with an inherently prideful nature so there is a limit to how far a human being will go on its own. When you see human beings who commit atrocities, the explanation is that they have been manipulated by outside forces into doing things that they naturally would not have done.

**If people learned how to free themselves from the influence of dark forces, we might actually be able to stop some of the incredible atrocities that are still occurring on a daily basis?**

Yes, but it would be especially valuable if people not only learned how to protect themselves from dark forces but also learned how to play an active role in removing dark forces from the planet. What keeps the dark forces on planet earth, and what gives them such power to manipulate human beings, is the fact that most people do not know how to protect themselves or call for the removal of dark spirits. I can assure you that we of the ascended masters have the power to remove all dark forces that are currently working on planet earth. Archangel Michael has legions of angels that could descend t earth and quickly bind all dark forces operating on this planet. Yet we do not have the authority to do so, and the explanation is the Law of Free Will.

It was the choices made by human beings that allowed the dark forces to enter this planet in the first place. Until human beings wake up, realize what is going on and decide to use their free will to reject the manipulation of dark forces, we of the ascended masters simply cannot remove these forces from the planet. This is explained in my parable about the tares among the wheat (Matthew 13:24-30). However, if human beings will wake up and come apart from the tares, then we can remove them very quickly.

When a human being invokes our protection or calls for the judgment of dark forces that person gives us the authority to remove the dark forces that are attacking him or her. If a critical mass of people would do this, we could quickly see a reduction in the number of dark beings operating on this planet. Thereby, many of the people who are not aware of the spiritual path would be set free from the influence of such dark forces. As a result, such people would stop committing some of the atrocities they are committing today. One of the most effective tools for protecting yourself and for removing dark forces from the planet is *Archangel Michael's Rosary*.

You are right that if all dark forces were removed from this planet, you would quickly see a dramatic reduction in the amount of atrocities that are occurring. Human beings would suddenly stop committing evil acts because they would now be free from the manipulation of the dark forces that trick so many people into doing evil without understanding what is

You might remember my statement on the cross: ive them; for they know not what they do" (Luke people do not know why they commit evil acts, not understand that they are being controlled by dark forces. If those dark forces were taken out of the equation, you would immediately see a dramatic improvement on planet earth.

Nevertheless, many people would still be in a lower state of consciousness that would make them prone to committing selfish acts so you would not instantly see the removal of all evil from this planet. That could only be done gradually, as people's consciousness was raised. Yet if the dark forces were removed from the planet, it would become much easier for human beings to raise their consciousness, and the planet would instantly enter an upward spiral that would quickly lead to better conditions.

It is entirely possible that the downward spiral of humankind could be turned around so that the earth could enter a golden age, which is what I called the "kingdom of God." The key ingredient is that human beings learn to use their free will to overcome the enemies without and the enemies within themselves.

### Some Christian churches claim that we are sinners by nature, are you saying that is not true?

Yes, that is exactly what I am saying. The problem with this Christian view is that if human beings were naturally sinners, they must have been created that way by God. Yet God is a God of unconditional love, and how could a God of love possibly create beings who by nature were prone to commit evil acts? This simply doesn't make sense when you think about it. Not even the beings who fell in a previous sphere were created to be evil. They were created by God and according to God's perfect vision. Yet God gave all self-aware beings free will, and therefore they have the potential to create a sense of identity that is out of alignment with God's original vision. This makes it possible for such beings to descend into a lower state of consciousness in which they do not see that they are performing evil acts. As I explain in *The Mystical Teachings of Jesus*, all so-called evil acts truly spring from ignorance.

I know this can be difficult to understand when you look at some of the atrocities committed by human beings. Yet it is a sad fact that the people who commit such acts believe the acts are necessary or justified according to a standard that they have created based on their own dualistic state of consciousness.

### How much of the evil that is occurring on this planet actually originated from dark forces?

In one sense you might say that all of it originated from dark forces. When you look at the story of the Garden of Eden, you will see that Adam and Eve were tempted by an outside force. The serpent in the Garden of Eden can be seen as a representative of the dark forces, the rebellious beings, that fell into the material universe from a previous sphere. Because they came here with the agenda to prove God wrong, they immediately started tempting people into misusing their free will.

Yet it would be incorrect to say that human beings are without responsibility for what has happened on earth. Human beings could only have been manipulated by the dark forces because they were vulnerable to temptation. They were vulnerable to this manipulation because they had misused their free will. There were many lifestreams in the Garden of Eden who did not fall for temptation, and these lifestreams have now permanently ascended to the spiritual realm. Those who fell for the temptation of the serpent ended up taking on a physical body on planet earth.

The original impulse was generated by dark spirits, yet it was the vulnerability in the psychology of human beings that made them respond to this manipulation. This is what I attempted to explain with the saying: "The Prince of this world comes and has nothing in me" (John 14:30). When you have incorrect beliefs or a selfish attitude, you become vulnerable to the manipulation of dark forces. I have said that the Law of Free Will is the ultimate law for this universe. The fact is that the dark forces cannot manipulate you unless you allow them to do so. They can manipulate you only because they have something in you that they can use as a tool for manipulation. You might have incorrect beliefs, a negative attitude or an accumulation of misqualified energy in your personal energy field. All of these factors can be used by the dark forces to control you and cause you to enter into a negative spiral that gradually causes you to lose control of your life and eventually self-destruct.

**What is the first step you recommend that people take in order to free themselves from the influence of dark forces?**

You first of all have to protect yourself from their influence, and the key to doing that is to invoke a wall of high-frequency spiritual energy around your mind and energy field. I am aware that many people will react with fear to these teachings about dark forces. The reason being that they think they cannot defend themselves. Yet remember that the dark forces cannot do anything with high-frequency spiritual energy. They can only use the low-frequency energies of the material realm.

Imagine that you are a medieval king sitting in his castle. You are being attacked by an mob of angry peasants, but they only have pitchforks and your castle has stone walls that are six feet thick. You can be completely comfortable inside your castle, because you know that pitchforks are no match for your stone walls. If you invoke a shield of high-frequency spiritual energy around your energy field, the dark forces will not be able to penetrate that shield. This can literally help you take back a greater measure of control of your life and reduce the amount of mental and emotional stress you feel.

Yet in the long run, invoking protection isn't enough in itself. You also need to resolve the imperfections in your psychology that cause you to be vulnerable to the manipulation and temptation of dark forces. One might say that using spiritual techniques can build a fortified wall around you, but your imperfect beliefs and attitudes are like windows in the wall. Obviously, the mob of angry peasants can throw their pitchforks through the windows in your castle walls and still hurt you even though they cannot get in.

**Speaking of getting in, what we have talked about so far is dark forces that are seeking to manipulate people from without, from outside their energy fields. Yet in the Bible there are examples of how you cast out evil spirits, and I assume these evil spirits had actually entered people's energy fields and were controlling them from the inside?**

That is correct, and it is entirely possible that a human being can have so many evil spirits in his or her energy field that the person has completely lost control. Yet I must say that if a person is open to the teachings in this book that person cannot be completely controlled by evil spirits. Such spirits would have prevented the person from ever reading this book. The people who are reading this book can take some consolation in this fact, but they still need to be aware that dark spirits can enter into their beings without taking full control.

In some cases, a dark spirit might reside in a person's energy field, but it only gains control over the person in certain situations. For example, some people manage to live relatively normal lives, but every once in awhile they give in to the desire to drink alcohol. As soon as such a person becomes drunk, it is almost as if you are dealing with a completely different person. The reason is that a dark spirit has now taken over the person's mind and actions. Once the influence of alcohol subsides, the person is back to his or her normal self as if nothing unusual had happened.

It is also possible that evil spirits can enter a person's energy field on a temporary basis and eventually be expelled again. People who go through traumatic situations, such as the loss of a loved one, a severe illness, losing a job or a divorce can be temporarily possessed by dark spirits that cause them to become depressed or angry. Yet after a while, the person's emotional body begins to heal and the dark forces cannot remain.

What can people do to protect themselves? Obviously, invoking spiritual protection makes it less likely that dark spirits can enter your energy field. If dark spirits are already in your field, invoking spiritual protection and spiritual energy will help expel the dark spirits. Such spirits cannot stand the vibration of high-frequency energy so as you invoke such energy, your energy field will become an uncomfortable abode for dark spirits.

As described in the Bible, I did cast out evil spirits, and I wish people would understand that everything I did and said was meant to demonstrate the path to Christhood that all human beings have the potential to follow. Because of the idolatry of my person created by orthodox Christianity, most people think that only someone outside themselves could cast out evil spirits. Yet the reality is that each person has a Christ self, which is a representative of the universal Christ mind for that person. As you walk the path of Christhood, you will gradually increase your conscious contact with your Christ self. Thereby, your Christ self can gradually descend into your energy field, and by doing so it will inevitably cast out any evil spirits in your field. When you put on the wedding garment of the Christ consciousness, you will become invulnerable to all dark spirits.

However, in order to fully put on that wedding garment and have the Conscious You unite with your Christ self, you must heal the wounds in your psychology that cause your lifestream to be vulnerable to dark forces.

**Are there certain places that have a higher concentration of evil spirits? I have always felt that some places are very uncomfortable whereas other places have a much purer vibration.**

Your feeling is correct, and many other people can intuitively sense the difference in vibration between various locations. For example, a prison often has a very negative vibration, as do many bars or places where people take drugs or perform various crimes.

You have no doubt heard the saying: "Men rush in where angels fear to tread." The meaning is that if human beings are not sensitive to vibration, they will rush into places that have a high concentration of misqualified energy. There are many places on earth where there is a vortex of negative psychic energy. Because dark forces feed off that energy, they are attracted to such locations. If you enter those places without spiritual protection, the energy itself will negatively affect your thoughts and feelings, and thereby you will become more vulnerable to evil spirits. Obviously, if you want to protect yourself from evil spirits, you will want to avoid such places if at all possible. If you cannot avoid such places, you need to be diligent and invoke spiritual protection so that you can enter without being dragged down by the energies and the dark spirits.

**Are there some cases where people would need the help of someone else in order to free themselves from evil spirits?**

Certainly. There are some ministers who are trained to perform exorcisms, and in extreme cases, they can be helpful. Yet unless we are talking about extreme cases, it would be more constructive for people to go to a professional therapist who specializes in a form of spirit release therapy. There are several forms of therapy that have been developed in recent years for this purpose, and they can be very effective, especially when people combine them with using the spiritual techniques I have mentioned.

**You talked about the fact that alcohol can be a factor in making people vulnerable to evil spirits. I assume that applies to other addictive substances as well?**

Of course. The nature of evil spirits is that they seek to control people, and the nature of addictive substances is that they cause you to lose control. The dark forces are constantly trying to manipulate people into taking addictive substances. When people become addicted, the dark forces can continually steal their energy. If a person dies from the addiction, the dark forces will simply move on to another victim. Any form of addictive substance and any form of addictive behavior, even addictive emotions, will make you vulnerable to dark forces. Basically, any addiction starts with the manipulation of dark forces. However, they can only manipulate you because you have already become vulnerable through psychological wounds or self-destructive beliefs. Once this vulnerability is created, the dark forces will move in and exploit it ruthlessly.

You must understand that such spirits are completely self-ish and have absolutely no regard for you or your life. They do not look at you as a human being but only as fodder, as an instrument they can use to get the energy they need. If given half a chance, evil spirits will mercilessly manipulate people until they slide into addiction, and the addiction then becomes a downward spiral from which people cannot free themselves.

## What can people do to overcome an addiction?

That depends somewhat on what kind of an addiction you are talking about. If the addiction involves a physical/chemical addiction, such as alcohol or smoking, you will need to treat both the body and mind. Once a chemical addiction has been established, you should use physical means to help the body recover from the chemical addiction. However, the chemical addiction was not the cause of the problem, because the addiction started in the mind. You must also treat addiction in the mind.

To successfully treat an addiction in the mind, I recommend adopting the attitude that you are literally fighting a battle for your soul. There is indeed an adversary, a villain, in this battle, namely dark forces that are seeking to prevent your spiritual progress through the addiction. The essence of an addiction is that it causes you to feel that you cannot move beyond a certain point, you cannot rise above a certain level on your spiritual path. The addiction is like a hook in your mind that pulls you back to a certain level or perhaps even takes you down lower.

In every addiction there is an enemy without and an enemy within. The enemy within is the human ego, and we will talk more about that later. The outer enemies are the dark spirits that we have been talking about in this chapter. What happens here is that an unholy alliance is formed between the human ego, which wants to hold you back and prevent you from uniting with your Christ self, and the outer forces, which want to keep you trapped in the material universe. If your Conscious You is not aware of these forces, it cannot protect itself effectively, and therefore it becomes an ignorant victim. To successfully fight such an attack, you need to use all the tools described in this book. You need to be diligent with spiritual protection and call for the binding of all imperfect forces that are attacking your soul, both from within and from without. You can call to Archangel Michael and myself to bind, consume and replace your ego. Call to the Elohim Astrea to cut you free from all dark forces and spirits. Use the tools given in the *Flowing With the River of Life Exercise Book*. You can also call for your Christ self to descend into your being and fill your consciousness and energy field with light so that there will be no room for any lower forces to enter. You can invoke spiritual energy to consume all imperfect energies stored in your energy field.

Yet in the end, the cause of any addiction is an imperfect belief about yourself, about God and about your relationship to God. To effectively overcome this belief, you need to consciously see the belief for what it is, namely a lie. You must then decide to replace that lie by making a better decision and affirm the reality that you are a son or daughter of God. This can best be done through attunement with your Christ self. Let me say that an essential element of any recovery from addiction is willpower. The addiction started with a decision you made, and it has been reinforced by many smaller decisions that all weaken your will to break the pattern. The essence of fighting any addiction is that you must strengthen your will to break the pattern. You can call for your Christ self and for me to reinforce your will, but the most efficient way to strengthen your will is through love. You must find something that you love so much that you realize the addiction is standing in the way of expressing or experiencing that love, and therefore you are willing to give up the addiction to reap the reward of what you love. You might love another person, a particular activity, your own soul, spiritual growth, me or God.

If you can find a love that is greater than the downward pull of the addiction, you have won half the victory. If you do not have such a point of love, use Mother Mary's invocations to call forth a miracle of her love filling your being. I can assure you that Mother Mary has love to spare, and she will be happy to give you a portion of her love. [Use the *Invocation for Clearing the Heart* and the *Invocation for Loving Yourself*, available on *www.transcendencetoolbox.com*.]

Another important tool is to realize that part of the addiction is a habit that has been created and reinforced by numerous repetitions of certain actions and thoughts. To break such a pattern will take time, and it is beneficial to make up short affirmations that affirm the positive decision you are using to replace the toxic decision. However, don't seek to overpower the old habit by creating a new one. Always ask your Christ self to consume the imperfect thoughts and feelings.

You might have heard the popular saying that what you resist persists. There is some truth to this, in the sense that if negative thoughts too much attention, you reinforce better to consciously surrender the thoughts to your f and ask it to consume them and to replace them with Christ truth. If you make an effort to build the habit of surrendering imperfect thoughts, you will have taken a major leap forward on your spiritual path.

All of these tools can be very effective, but in order to successfully fight a serious addiction, it is necessary to take a long-term approach. The decision that led to the present addiction might have been made in a past life. You cannot expect that such an addiction can be resolved overnight. It might indeed take years to get to the bottom of such a problem.

In some cases, depending on how severe the addiction is, it will be strongly advisable to seek the help of a skilled professional. There are many forms of therapy that can help you get to the bottom of the dysfunctional decision behind the addiction. Because the science of psychology is currently based on a materialistic view of the world, traditional psychotherapy is not the best tool available. There are a number of new and alternative psychological healing methods that are far better.

To determine whether to make use of such therapy, follow the impulses you get from your heart. If you decide to engage in therapy, use the spiritual tools to prepare for your sessions and to follow up. Spend some time using the spiritual tools to call for protection and the transformation of toxic energies. Then do as many sessions as needed until you feel you have gained greater clarity. In between sessions, use the spiritual tools. Call for the binding of any inner and outer forces that are standing in your way. Use the Violet Flame or Mother Mary's invocations to consume any imperfect energies that are brought up during the sessions. If you will combine therapy and spiritual tools, you can make much faster progress, and you might indeed be amazed at the results.

You live at a time when valuable tools have been brought forth in many areas of life. There is absolutely no reason to ignore these tools because they can speed up your progress on the spiritual path. Let me say that I am amazed that people will look backward and think that in order to follow Christ, they should live the way I or my disciples lived 2,000 years ago. This really is not my recommendation. I can assure you that I would have made use of any type of beneficial technology if it had been available when I walked this planet.

### Anything else you want to say about dark spirits?

Yes, a wise man, Saint Thomas More, once said: "The devil, the proud spirit, cannot endure to be mocked." You should always remember that dark spirits have great pride, and they take themselves very seriously. If you do not take yourself too seriously, you will be much less vulnerable to the influence of dark spirits. Many people are caught up in pride or other self-centered attitudes, and it opens their souls to the manipulation by dark spirits who are masters at using people's pride as weapons against them.

In many cases, a bit of humor can be the best defense against dark spirits, and that also applies to overcoming your fear of such spirits. Fear is another emotion that is used very skillfully by dark spirits. For thousands of years, they have used fear to control the people of earth, and they have often used religion to create this fear. This is a tragedy and a travesty that I would like to see corrected. I encourage all people on the spiritual path to establish a connection to their Christ selves so they can accept the flow of perfect love, meaning God's unconditional love, that will cast out all of their fears. Once again, the key to overcoming dark spirits is to always respond with love. When you respond with love, the prince of this world has nothing in you. When you respond with humor, you have something in him.

# 10 | RISE ABOVE DIFFICULT SITUATIONS

I know this might be a bit repetitive, but I feel it is important to cover the topic from another angle. I have met many people who have been exposed to severe abuse or trauma in this lifetime, and some of these people are open to the need to heal their psychology. Others will not change until they experience a crisis that forces them to change, and I think part of the reason is that when we have been exposed to trauma, we can lose our willpower and our ability to take control over our lives. This can then lead to addictions, as we just talked about.

You were also saying that all of us probably have scars from past lives so it sounds to me like all of us could benefit from knowing how to heal such trauma. What are your suggestions for how to overcome trauma and take back control of our lives?

It is difficult to give a general answer to a question like this. The reason being that there are so many individual factors at play. There can be several reasons a lifestream is exposed to severe abuse, and there are many different scenarios for how such abuse affects the soul. Let me focus on the type of lifestreams who are most likely to read this book.

The type of lifestreams who are likely to be attracted to this book are people who have reached a more advanced level of maturity and are on the path to personal Christhood. These are precisely the type of lifestreams that are a threat to the dark forces who are working against God's vision for humankind and for individual lifestreams. As I said, when you begin to manifest your Christhood, you will become a target for dark forces.

One of the plots used by such forces is to create the greatest possible amount of chaos in your childhood so that your life's mission is distorted or even aborted at the outset. In their attempts to do this, dark forces will seek to take over weak-minded individuals around you and use them to expose you to severe abuse. Obviously, I am not saying that all people who are abused are on the path to Christhood or that every lifestream on the path will necessarily be abused. If you have been abused as a child and if you are open to the teachings in this book, you should consider yourself to be an advanced lifestream. You should consider that the abuse you experienced was a direct attack on your lifestream, precipitated by dark forces. Even if you have not been abused in this life, you could have been exposed to abuse in past lives and still need healing.

Based on this recognition, I hope people will reach the conclusion that you cannot allow anything that happened to you in this world to stand in the way of the goal of manifesting your Christhood and fulfilling your spiritual mission for this lifetime. I hope people will make the decision to pursue any avenue possible in order to heal the wounds they received in childhood – or in past lives – and leave them permanently behind so they can get on with their mission and Christhood.

If you will make this decision, and if you will follow through by taking advantage of all avenues of healing, you will find that there will be an extraordinary help and support from Above. Contrary to what you might have been taught as you were growing up, or what you might have concluded as a result of the abuse, you are not alone. You have a Christ self and you have angels and ascended beings assigned to help your lifestream overcome all obstacles and manifest your Christhood. If you will call to us with an open mind, you will receive the help and guidance you need in order to take the next step toward healing.

The first practical step toward putting childhood abuse (or any type of abuse) behind you is to recognize the fact that the abuse was an attack on your lifestream by dark forces. This should make it obvious that you need to make a very determined effort to establish or reestablish your spiritual protection. This involves making diligent use of appropriate techniques for spiritual protection, as mentioned earlier.

The next practical step you can take is to recognize that when you are exposed to severe trauma and abuse, especially when it happens in childhood, it is virtually inevitable that your soul vehicle will become fragmented, as we will discuss later. The tools that will help you heal psychological wounds will also help you heal a fragmented soul. It will also be a great help to study both spiritual teachings and books on spirituality and psychology. You can also find techniques for healing the soul or the inner child. For example, *Mother Mary's East-West Invocation* is specifically designed to heal a fragmented soul. Yet in the end it will be highly beneficial for people who have endured severe abuse to enter some form of therapy with a trained professional. I earlier described some of the forms of therapy that can be beneficial.

I would also strongly recommend that you contemplate the possibility that your lifestream might have chosen to embody in a situation where there was a high probability of abuse. There are several reasons your lifestream might have made this choice. One is that you wanted to learn a specific lesson that would help you resolve something in your psychology. If this is the case, it is extremely important that you discover what that lesson is and fully integrate the lesson into your being. Another potential reason is that you wanted to learn the lesson that you cannot rely on anything or anybody outside of yourself but that you must go within and establish contact to your Christ self.

Another reason for choosing a difficult childhood is that you are a mature lifestream who wants to help other people. You chose to do this by experiencing a very difficult situation yourself so that you know what it feels like and can therefore be more effective in helping others overcome the negative effects of abuse. However, to fulfill your mission to help others, you must heal yourself.

Finally, your lifestream might have chosen a situation that could lead to abuse because you wanted to bring the judgment upon certain souls that have committed abuses in the past. You should consider it your right and your obligation to call forth God's judgment upon the people who abused you and all the dark forces working through them. This is indeed one of the reasons I allowed myself to be crucified. In committing this abuse against a person with full Christhood, these lifestreams, and the dark forces working through them, brought about their own judgment. Although the very act of abuse is a judgment, it is still beneficial to call forth the judgment.

Another very important step is to work on enveloping the entire situation in the flame of forgiveness. *Mother Mary's*

*Miracle Forgiveness Rosary* is a powerful tool for doing this. Mother Mary has given teachings on forgiveness, [See *www. ascendedmasterlight.com*] and it is extremely important to study them because the only way to leave the abuse behind is to fully forgive those who abused you. To fully forgive, you need to separate the person and the acts. People commit abusive acts because of wounds in their psyches that make them vulnerable to dark forces. When you realize this, you can forgive the person, even if you cannot forgive the act. I am not asking you to look at abusive acts as somehow acceptable—they are never acceptable. I am only asking you to forgive the person who committed such acts out of ignorance.

It is also important that you forgive yourself for your reaction to the abuse or anything you might have done as a result of the abuse. As a child, most people tend to think that if something bad happens to them, they must have done something to cause it. This makes many children accept a false sense of responsibility for the actions of the adults around them. In reality, the child was not responsible for the actions of the adults; the adults were acting out their own unresolved psychology, and they were likely influenced or controlled by dark forces.

An unfortunate effect of the Christian doctrine about sin is that many children feel that if they were abused, they must have committed a sin that made them deserve this abuse and this might mean that they are bad people. It is extremely important for you to overcome such negative feelings about yourself, and you can do so only by fully forgiving yourself—not so much for the abuse as for your reaction to the abuse or any actions, such as an attempt to dull the pain with alcohol or drugs, that followed the abuse.

The dark forces try to trap you in a limited self image that makes you feel you could never again be worthy to come home to God. This can put you in a spiritual Catch-22 from which it can be very difficult to recover until you see through the methods and the intent of dark forces. The most unfortunate effect of severe abuse is that a child can feel that it has been so violated by the abuse that it could never again be worthy to face God. This is the ultimate lie used by dark forces, and it is extremely important that you see through this lie, accept it as a lie and consciously dismiss it. You must accept the fact that there is nothing that could possibly have happened to you in this world that you cannot overcome and leave behind.

It is also important to understand the correct relationship between the Conscious You, your soul and your I AM Presence. Your Conscious You never had dominion over your I AM Presence, and it is not meant to have such dominion. When the Conscious You is connected to your I AM Presence, your Presence has dominion over your Conscious You and soul. You need to let your Presence take back dominion over your being, and you do that by healing your soul and reestablishing the connection to your Christ self and through that to your I AM Presence.

I realize that when a person has been deeply wounded, it can be very painful to think about the entire situation surrounding the abuse. It can therefore be very difficult for such a lifestream to realize and acknowledge the truth in Mother Mary's teaching that nobody ever did anything to you. What she is really saying is that although someone abused you as a child, what caused your soul to be hurt was not the outer act of abuse but your reaction to it. This might be difficult to accept until your soul has been somewhat healed.

When you have been abused, it is almost inevitable that the soul vehicle (the four levels of the mind) will have fractured and that some of the fragments have become separated from your soul. This leaves empty spaces within the structure of your soul, and those empty spaces can be filled by impure energies or even by dark spirits that seek to control your life. Because there is not enough soul substance left after the abuse and because of outside forces manipulating your soul, it can feel as if your will was taken away from you. The reason being that the soul substance that is left might not be strong enough to take dominion over the structure of your soul. Yet as you begin to put on spiritual protection, and as you begin to heal your soul, you will magnetize some of the lost soul fragments back to you and you will expel the foreign energies and beings. This will gradually build a critical mass, and you will eventually reach a point of greater wholeness where you can take back dominion over your will.

However, I must make it clear that this is not an automatic process. The brutal fact is that no force in this world can take away your will. When the forces of this world expose you to severe trauma and abuse, your lifestream is in such turmoil that it can voluntarily give away its will. The lifestream can feel it has made such a severe mistake, that it has been so wounded or that its situation is so chaotic that it could not possibly do anything on its own to resolve the situation.

The lifestream can voluntarily give up its will. As you begin the process of healing, there will come a point where you have magnetized enough soul fragments that you are able to take back your will. Yet taking back your will must be a conscious decision. You can take back your will only through an act of will. You gave it away through an act of will, and you must take it back the same way.

There are serpentine lies designed to make you believe that if only you engage in a certain outer ritual, you will automatically be healed. The outer ritual of healing can indeed help you heal your soul. But in the end, you must consciously take back your will by making the decision to accept full accountability for your own situation.

Please understand that I fully realize how difficult it can be for a person who has been severely abused, or who has been exposed to other forms of trauma, to feel any kind of personal responsibility for the situation. I am not asking you to feel accountable for what other people did to you. Nor am I asking you to feel that you must be a bad person to have such things happen to you. I am asking you to accept accountability for your reaction to the situation so that you accept the fact that what hurt your soul was the decisions you made – the false self-image you accepted – while the abuse was taking place or afterward. I am then asking you to accept the fact that those decisions were the best possible decisions you could have made at the time, given your state of consciousness and maturity. This should be especially obvious concerning abuse that happened during childhood, but it truly applies to everyone.

I am then asking you to accept that because you have now reached a higher level of maturity, you could have made better decisions today than you made back then. When you come to this recognition, you can allow yourself to re-experience the situation and replace the original decision with a better decision. I recognize that this can be painful, but if you go through the steps of establishing spiritual protection and transforming toxic energies, the pain will be much less intense.

The damage that was done to your soul was done through decisions you made. The only way the damage can be permanently undone is by you making better decisions that replace the old choices. Once again, the help of an experienced therapist can be invaluable in terms of helping you go through the difficult process of facing your past decisions and replacing them with better ones.

I also realize it might take a long time to fully heal the effects of childhood abuse. Yet I can assure you that no matter what might have happened to you, it is possible to leave it all behind and manifest your personal Christhood. I can also promise you that by making the effort to seek healing, you will reap a reward that will make it all worth it. Once you are free from such past trauma, you will feel spiritually reborn, and you can then begin to express your Christhood and fulfill your divine plan.

Incidentally, your mission in life might be to help other victims of abuse and show them how to be healed. Or it might be to increase awareness about abuse and help society put an end to it—which must include a greater understanding of the spiritual causes of abuse, including the existence of dark forces.

**I can attest from my own life that when I started using spiritual techniques for protection and the transformation of toxic energy, I gained a lot more control over my emotions. As a result, it also became much easier for me to deal with challenging situations and to respond to such situations with love. Yet I am still wondering if you have a suggestion for how people can deal with life's more difficult situations in a way that helps them grow?**

I would recommend that you adopt the attitude that everything that happens to you is an opportunity for growth. Even life's most difficult situations offer you an opportunity to learn something about life and about your own psychology. Any situation can be used as an opportunity to let go of some element of the death consciousness or some attachment to the things of this world.

I want to make it clear that I am not hereby saying that everything that happens to you is acceptable according to some ultimate standard. It is not correct to say that if someone abuses you, it is just an opportunity for you to learn, and therefore abuse fits into the great scheme of things. Abuse, violence and other types of unkind behavior is not part of God's plan or vision for this universe. You should approach every situation as an opportunity for you to grow, regardless of what other people do or how they respond to the situation. In that respect, it is extremely important to understand the Law of Cause and Effect. According to this law, no one can escape the consequences of their actions. If someone abuses you that person will make personal karma and the person can never escape having to balance that karma.

When you understand how exact God's law is, you can overcome one of the major stumbling blocks on the spiritual path. If you look at history, you will see that millions of people have allowed themselves to be dragged into drawn-out conflicts with other people. In many cases, such a conflict started because one person did something wrong to another. However, the second person now entered a state of consciousness in which he or she felt that it was necessary to punish the first person. When people enter that state of consciousness, when they respond with anger, hatred or the desire for revenge, they are actually punishing themselves.

When you seek revenge over another, you will inevitably misqualify God's energy and produce negative karma for yourself. In that respect, it is truly of no significance what the other person has done to you. The other person has already incurred his or her personal karma for those actions. God's law has already made sure that the person will reap a just reward. It is not necessary for you to inflict punishment upon the other person because that person has already created his or her own punishment. God's law will ensure that the punishment is meted out. It might not happen in this lifetime but it will inevitably happen. Many people have allowed themselves to be trapped in a negative karmic spiral in which both sides seek revenge. This creates an ongoing spiral which can develop into family feuds or wars between nations. When you realize the reality of reincarnation, you see that some people bind themselves to reembody with the same people over and over again. If someone abuses you, why would you want to create a karmic spiral with that person? Why would you want to reincarnate with that person over many lifetimes? If someone is abusive, why not simply leave that person behind and move on to better things?

How can you leave an abusive person behind? Follow my advice to turn the other cheek. If a person abuses you, the person will make karma. If you respond with anger, hatred or a desire for revenge, you will also make karma. However, if you remain non-attached and turn the other cheek, you will not make karma from the situation. You will not be pulled into a conflict, and therefore you will not create a karmic tie between yourself and the abusive person. When you do turn the other cheek, you will have won a significant victory on your personal path.

My purpose for giving this explanation is to help people see that even though some of the things that happen to you are not right according to God's law, they are still an opportunity for growth. If you will turn the other cheek, you can grow from even the most difficult situations.

### Do you have a suggestion that can help us respond to difficult situations in a more positive manner?

Your first concern should be to avoid creating negative karma for yourself. You must turn the other cheek and avoid responding to the situation with negative feelings, such as anger or a desire for revenge. I realize that before you can truly turn the other cheek, you must have reached a certain point of inner resolution. You must fully understand and accept that life is an opportunity for growth. To reach this inner resolution will require an effort, but it will also require an understanding of how life really works in the material universe. Let me attempt to give you a brief overview of this topic.

I fully understand that so many people feel like they are victims of circumstances beyond their control. One of the most common questions asked by people who encounter a difficult situation is: "Why did this happen to me?" Most people feel that they could never possibly have chosen the difficult challenges they face in life. While this reaction is understandable, I must tell you that it is often incorrect.

As I have stated many times, human beings have created the current conditions on planet earth. They have created these conditions by making imperfect choices and thereby misqualifying God's energy. By doing so, people have created personal karma, and this karma acts as a magnet that draws their lifestreams back to the material universe. I fully understand that when you are in embodiment and enveloped in a difficult situation, it is hard to see that situation as a result of your own choices. The reason is that when the lifestream is in embodiment, it often becomes overpowered by or absorbed in its outer circumstances. Yet when the lifestream is out of embodiment, the lifestream escapes this involvement and is able to look at its situation from a higher and less emotional perspective. There are several books on the market that describe the situation encountered by lifestreams between lifetimes or during near-death experiences. I highly recommend that people study such books.

Before a lifestream comes into embodiment, the lifestream meets with its spiritual teachers and creates a plan for that particular lifetime. Because the lifestream is not overpowered by outer circumstances, it can take a long-term perspective and make decisions that are aimed at helping it rise to a higher level on its personal path. When the lifestream plans its next embodiment, it often chooses to embody in circumstances that offer maximum opportunity for spiritual growth. When I talk about the maximum opportunity for growth, I do not mean that the lifestream chooses circumstances in which everything is easy and comfortable. Contrary to popular belief, any lifestream that descends to planet earth is a courageous lifestream. The current conditions on this planet are very difficult, and it takes a great deal of courage for a lifestream to embody here. Most spiritual people are courageous lifestreams who are determined to learn their lessons and move on with life. They often deliberately choose circumstances that present major challenges or give them an opportunity to balance personal karma. There are literally millions of examples of how courageous lifestreams have chosen to embody in the most difficult situations imaginable. The reason being that these particular circumstances give the lifestream the best opportunity to grow and balance karma.

The essence of growth is that you leave behind your attachments to a limited image of yourself and the world. A lifestream will often choose to embody in circumstances that force it to deal with some of its limitations and attachments. The lifestream knows that once it is in a physical body, it is very tempting to seek to avoid challenges and difficulties. Many people spend a lifetime trying to avoid challenges or make themselves comfortable, yet this often prevents the lifestream from learning its lessons and therefore progressing on the path. A lifestream often chooses a set of circumstances that are so difficult that it becomes harder for it to ignore its attachments. For example, imagine a lifestream who, over many lifetimes, has allowed people to abuse it. The lifestream has refused to stand up for itself and draw the line. Such a lifestream might choose to embody as the daughter of an abusive father. By being unable to escape the abuse of its father, the lifestream gains the maximum opportunity to finally stand up for itself, draw a line in the sand and say: "Thus far and no farther!"

**I understand what you are saying, and I agree that when you accept that you have chosen your circumstances in life, it becomes easier to accept those circumstances and make the best use of them. But I still don't think this is enough to help people deal with personal tragedy. When you experience tragedy, it is so easy to be overwhelmed by the emotions. How can you best deal with that?**

Once again, I would like people to consider that I had great compassion for people's suffering. My entire ministry sprang from that compassion. That is why I so often healed the sick and attempted to comfort those who suffered emotional pain. I would also like people to understand that my mission was not a feel-good ministry. To use a modern expression, I was not attempting to enable people to remain in their current state of consciousness. I was attempting to empower people to come up higher and experience the abundant life.

There is a very important difference between human sympathy, which seeks to make people feel good about remaining in a bad situation, and true empathy that seeks to help people rise above their limitations. A true spiritual teacher will always seek to empower the students to come up higher in consciousness. I am saying this because I truly feel great compassion for the millions of people who are suffering ongoing afflictions or temporary tragedies. I do not want such people to feel that I am insensitive to their suffering. Yet this is a book and I cannot show personal empathy for each person who reads the book. My aim here is to show people how they can avoid being trapped in negative feelings by using tragedy as a stepping stone on their path.

You are quite right that when you experience personal tragedy, it is easy to be overwhelmed by emotional energy. In that respect, it is important for people to realize that when you are on planet earth, you are literally swimming in an ocean of toxic emotional energy. Your personal energy field is like a drop in that ocean of energy. If you do not take measures to protect your personal energy field, it is easy to become overwhelmed by the energy that surrounds you. When you experience a personal tragedy, it is easy to open your energy field to a flood of emotional energy that literally sweeps you away. This is why some people become overwhelmed by sorrow over the loss of a loved one or sink into a permanent state of depression from which there seemingly is no escape. These people are simply overwhelmed by the emotional energy of the mass consciousness. In some cases, such emotional energy can be directed at you by dark forces who are seeking to derail your spiritual progress. I must, once again, stress the importance of spiritual protection against this emotional energy.

It will also be helpful to realize that dark forces have always used the emotions as an inroad for controlling people. Emotions are, by their nature, fluid and easy to manipulate. You need to be vigilant in protecting your emotional body from the onslaughts of the world. You need to internalize and apply the teachings I gave earlier about the connection between emotions, thoughts and your sense of identity. Once you begin to change your sense of identity and accept that you are a spiritual being who has chosen your circumstances, your outlook on life will begin to change.

Most people have a subtle expectation that life should be easy and trouble-free. This expectation is programmed into their minds by dark forces who have created a materialistic culture. It holds up an ideal of a rich, young, beautiful and trouble-free person and tells people that this is the way life should be. The dark forces then seek to manipulate people into difficult situations that violate the expectations they have created. The purpose – apart from selling you a product or service that you don't need – is to derail your growth and cause you to generate misqualified energy. Instead of this false image, people should see life as an opportunity for growth and learn from their difficulties instead of seeking to buy their way out of them.

When many people encounter difficult situations, their first thought is that the situation is wrong, that it is somehow unjust and that they are victims of the situation. The second thought is how they can escape the situation without changing their attitude to life. When you accept that you are a spiritual being and that you have chosen your circumstances, these thoughts are replaced with more constructive thoughts. You will not have the general expectation that life should be easy and trouble-free. You will naturally see challenges as an opportunity for growth, and you will look for the hidden lesson. You will seek to learn that lesson instead of seeking to escape the discomfort of the situation. You will be willing to change yourself, to change your attitude and increase your understanding of life. You will be willing to endure a temporary discomfort in order to learn a lesson and win a permanent victory.

You might even realize that if the situation causes you emotional pain that pain is caused by one thing only, namely an attachment. The stronger the attachment, the stronger the emotional pain. The emotional pain can be used as a tool for uncovering your attachments, and when you overcome an attachment, the emotional pain will be gone. The emotional pain will not be suppressed; the attachment that generated the pain will be permanently resolved and removed. Once you develop a constructive approach to life, you will escape the negative thoughts and the painful emotions that people experience as a result of personal tragedy. Your actions will be more balanced, and you can avoid responding to a personal crisis in a way that sets the stage for the next crisis.

**Let us say that a person has gone through a very difficult personal crisis and feels drained of energy and worn out. The person attempts to pray but cannot find any inner peace or connection to God. What could such a person do to get back on a positive track in life?**

You can begin by recognizing the reality of the situation, and the reality is that you have been wounded and need healing. I see so many people who get hurt emotionally, yet they have no idea how to heal themselves. It is one of the great lacks in Western culture that people are not brought up with an understanding of how to heal their energy fields and psychology. All of this will change in the coming decades, but that does little to help you now. You need to recognize that as your body can get hurt, so can your energy field, meaning your emotional, mental and identity bodies.

If you had broken a leg, there is no question that you would go to the hospital. You would also have to spend some time to let the leg heal before you could go on with your normal routine. The problem is that most people do not recognize that their energy fields can be hurt, as can their bodies. When your energy field is hurt, you need to break off from your daily routine, take care of yourself and heal your mental and emotional bodies just as you would heal the physical body. Yet most people think that if you get hurt emotionally, you should be able to carry on your daily responsibilities as if nothing had happened.

If you break a leg, you do not expect that you can run a marathon until it is healed. Likewise, if you have severely damaged your energy field by going through a traumatic experience, you should not expect to go on with your daily activities without making an effort to heal yourself.

When you find it difficult to pray and meditate, or in other ways connect to God, it is because your energy field has been damaged. Your field is therefore open to toxic energies or dark spirits, and they are streaming into your field. They can overpower your thoughts and feelings, making it difficult to meditate or even pray. You need to be very conscious of the fact that you should take time to heal your energy field, just as you would heal your body.

You will need rest to heal your energy field, but rest does not necessarily mean inactivity. If you break a leg, you do need to keep it still, but the inevitable side effect is that your muscles become weak. To heal your energy field, you need to stop activities that cause you strain, such as certain parts of your daily routine, but you should not simply become inactive or passive. I recommend that you set aside as many of your normal activities as you can, and then engage in a set ritual that you follow every day. If you were sick and had to take medicine, there would be no doubt in your mind that you would take that medicine twice a day as prescribed by the doctor. When it comes to healing your energy field, you need spiritual medicine. You need to make a decision that you will engage in a specific spiritual ritual and that you will perform the ritual every day. You simply make a firm decision that you will perform a specific ritual and that you will keep doing so for a certain period of time, such as two or three weeks.

I realize that people feel exhausted after a traumatic experience, and the thought of performing a ritual can seem overwhelming. Yet in reality, your emotional body will welcome the ritual because it will help reestablish the order and integrity of your energy field. After all, it was the chaos and irregularity of the negative experience that caused the trauma. The key to healing is not to simply refrain from all activity. The key is to reestablish order, and a ritual is the best way to do this.

What can seem overwhelming is the thought of making decisions and having to perform the ritual daily. That is why I suggest approaching it as if the doctor had prescribed medicine for a physical illness. In that case, the decision is made out of necessity, and once a firm decision is made, there is no stress about it. You simply have to do it. In performing a spiritual ritual every day, you will build a positive spiral that will eventually heal your energy field and once again seal it from the toxic energies that make you unable to pray or meditate.

When I say spiritual ritual, I do not mean a ritual that requires you to think or even concentrate. I am talking about a ritual that you can follow in an almost mechanical manner until you are healed and can once again start putting more heart into the ritual. Although many of our decrees and invocations work, the absolutely most powerful tool for healing a severe trauma is *The Song of Life Healing Matrix* released by the representatives of the Divine Mother. [See *www.morepublish. com.*] There is simply nothing else that compares to its power to heal psychological trauma and physical illness.

If you will perform such a ritual religiously, you will begin to see an improvement, and you will again be able to feel connected to God. Let me also say that while you are going through this process of healing, you should not worry about feeling connected to God. If your energy field has been bruised or damaged, it will be very difficult for you to feel connected. Simply be unconcerned about this and perform the ɪ you spontaneously feel that your connection is con If you perform the ritual every day, your connection back. Yet if you start stressing about not feeling connected to God, you will only make the situation worse. That is why I recommend a ritual that you can follow mechanically until your energy field regains enough wholeness to reestablish the connection to God.

### Why do we encounter conditions that seem like they will never change?

There are two main reasons. One is that the situation represents an opportunity to learn a lesson in life. Until the lifestream learns the lesson, the situation will not change. This is not the result of some kind of magic. In many cases, a situation will not change until a person takes certain actions. Because of the person's psychological limitations, he or she will not be able to take those actions until the lifestream has learned the lesson it needs to learn from the situation.

Another reason is that the situation is the result of the person's karma from past lives. In many cases, a specific condition, such as an illness, can be an efficient way to pay back karma and thereby achieve greater freedom in the future. The lifestream might have chosen such circumstances in order to accelerate the paying back of karma. The condition will not change until the karma is fully balanced, or paid back. However, I can assure you that there are far better ways to balance karma than to experience disease or other unpleasant circumstances.

If you are facing difficult circumstances and want them to change, I recommend that you engage in a rigorous program of applying a spiritual technique for balancing karma, especially the Violet Flame and Mother Mary's invocations. At the same time, do everything possible to penetrate your psychology and find out what lesson you need to learn from the situation. Almost every situation you encounter in life is a product of both karma and the need to learn a lesson. By attacking the problem on both fronts, you will shorten the time it takes to reach a resolution whereby the situation can be changed.

Millions of people have experienced that, after walking the spiritual path for a while, they are suddenly free of conditions that had followed them for decades. In reality, those conditions might have followed you for lifetimes. After you experience how seemingly never-ending circumstances are suddenly gone, you are likely to renew your commitment to the spiritual path.

### What would you say to people who ask: "Why did this happen to me?"

I would ask them to consider why people always ask that question. Why is it that almost every person who experiences a tragedy instinctively asks why this happened? One of the biggest obstacles on the spiritual path is the sense that you are a victim of circumstances beyond your control. One of the major turning points on the path is when the lifestream realizes that it has created its own situation and that it must uncreate it. The very fact that people always ask why certain things happen to them demonstrates that the lifestream has an inner knowing that it is not a victim of circumstances beyond its control. The lifestream knows that the universe is not random or arbitrary. The lifestream knows that the universe is guided by laws and that there are reasons why certain things happen. The lifestream also knows that once it discovers those reasons, it will gain the power to change its circumstances.

My reaction would be to encourage people to use the question as a launchpad for a journey toward a deeper understanding of life and of themselves. By increasing their understanding, they will increase their power to improve their circumstances and prevent undesirable things from happening to them. Let me give a brief summary of why certain things happen to people:

- An event might be an opportunity to learn. A lifestream might have chosen a specific circumstance because it wanted to force itself to learn certain lessons. The best way to change the circumstance is to learn the lesson and resolve the psychological wounds.

- An event might be the result of returning karma from past lives. Welcome the opportunity to balance that karma and use spiritual tools to balance the karma as quickly as possible.

- An event might be the consequence of a choice you made in this lifetime. It has nothing to do with karma or a previous choice. However, it will spring from a decision that is the result of your current psychology. Use the situation as an opportunity to resolve your psychological issues so you can make better choices.

- An event might be the result of another person misusing his or her free will. Use the situation as an opportunity to strengthen your ability to respond to all situations with love. Pray for the other person to be protected and enlightened.

- An event might be a direct attack on your lifestream precipitated by dark forces. In many cases, such forces will use weak-minded people to carry out the attack. Use spiritual protection, call forth the judgment of the dark forces and take appropriate actions to protect yourself.

Obviously, you did not choose situations caused by other people or dark forces. Yet in a sense you did indirectly choose the circumstances because you made the decision to embody on planet earth. On this planet, most people are in a lower state of consciousness and there are dark forces roaming the world. Your lifestream knew that and took a calculated risk by coming here. Even if an event is not by your own choosing, it can still be viewed as an opportunity. You have the opportunity to turn the other cheek and to prove that you can be who you are and respond with love even though you are being mistreated by other people.

There is a very fine balance to find in considering why things happen to you. As discussed earlier, some Eastern religions have developed a very fatalistic view of life, stating that whatever happens to you is the result of your past karma. This is similar to Western people believing everything is the result of God's will or the workings of a machine. Yet, as I have just explained, many aspects of your life are not predetermined.

Many aspects of your life are determined by your choices and by the choices of other people. When you develop an uncompromising respect for free will, you will allow other people to make their choices and accept that God has given them the right to make those choices. You will accept that when you made the choice to embody on earth, you took a calculated risk, and you might indeed be exposed to abuse from other people.

You will also realize that by maintaining respect for your own free will, you can be who you are regardless of how you are treated by others. Because this is the essential challenge for anyone walking the spiritual path, one might say that even when other people misuse their free will, they still give you an opportunity to grow.

If a situation is meant to teach you a lesson, you can change that situation by learning the lesson. If a situation is the result of your past karma, you can change that situation by balancing the karma. However, if a situation is the result of other people's choices, you might not be able to change those choices and thereby change the outer situation. Yet you can still use that situation to further your personal progress by changing the way you respond to the situation. You will quickly realize that if you remain non-attached to the outer situation and remain true to who you are, a crisis can work itself out as if by magic. You will also begin to encounter fewer and fewer of such situations.

One might say that the spiritual path is a process of gaining self-mastery. An important part of this mastery is that you gain control over your reactions to other people and to the situations you encounter in life. Most people do not have such control because they have subconscious computer programs, emotional wounds, vortexes of toxic energies or evil spirits that prevent them from choosing their reaction to most situations. The reaction to a given situation is predetermined by the subconscious limitations and the person cannot override it with the conscious mind. As you walk the path, you will gradually remove these subconscious limitations and gain control over your four lower bodies. Thereby, you will increase your ability to consciously choose your reaction to situations. You will gain the inner peace and non-attachment that empowers you to make the free, conscious choice to respond to all situations with love. This is true self-mastery!

**I assume this teaching can be applied to the old question of why prayer isn't always answered?**

That is correct. Everything is subject to free will so God will not answer a prayer that would violate someone's free will, including your own. Here are the most common reasons why a prayer isn't answered:

• When a person is going through a difficult situation, the person often prays for God to take away the pain by miraculously changing the situation. Yet that prayer comes from the person's surface consciousness, or the conscious mind. It will not override a decision made at the deeper levels of the lifestream. For example, if the lifestream has chosen to embody in certain circumstances in order to learn a specific lesson, God will not answer a prayer to remove the pain of those circumstances. If God did remove the pain, the lifestream could ignore the situation and thereby miss the opportunity to learn its lesson. Instead of praying for the pain to go away, pray for inner direction to help your lifestream learn its lesson. You will be amazed at how the ascended masters will respond to such a prayer, especially if you have a sincere desire for a higher understanding and a willingness to look beyond your present beliefs. It is beneficial to acknowledge that there can be a difference, sometimes a vast difference, between what the lifestream wants at deeper levels and what a person wants at the surface level of consciousness.

• In some cases, a difficult situation is precipitated by the person's karma. The karma is the person's responsibility because it is a result of its past choices. God will not simply remove the pain of that karma as the result of a prayer because doing so would prevent the lifestream from learning the basic lesson that it must take responsibility for its own choices, past, present and future. Use spiritual techniques to transform the karma instead of asking God to do the work for you.

• In many cases, people pray for God to change other people. However, doing so would interfere with these people's free will. God will not answer your prayer if doing so violates your soul's choices or the Law of Free Will. Resolve your psychological wounds so you can be non-attached and respond to others with love.

• In some cases, you might have chosen to embody with a particular person in order to help that lifestream make progress on the path. If the person is difficult to deal with, avoid responding with negative feelings. Instead, use spiritual tools to call for the person to be protected and enlightened. Educate yourself so that you might help the person attain a greater understanding of life.

The main problem with understanding how prayer works is that religions have for so long promoted an incorrect image of God. Many religions portray God as an infallible, all-powerful being. Many people feel that if God was less than perfect or not all-powerful, their faith in God and religion would be destroyed. The key to overcoming this impasse is to fully acknowledge the Law of Free Will. God has given people free will and will not violate his own law. If you pray for something that would violate your free will or the free will of another human being, God will not answer your prayer. God is not, as many people seem to think, an arbitrary being who saves some and condemns others to eternal damnation. God is a rational being who has created laws according to which people choose to save or condemn themselves.

Let us take these considerations to a higher level. We are entering an age in which human beings must come to a higher understanding of themselves. We are entering an age in which people are meant to see themselves as co-creators with God. When I appeared 2,000 years ago, I presented an image of God as a loving father figure. This was the image that was meant to guide people over the past 2,000 years. During that age, it was acceptable and necessary that people prayed for God to do something for them. However, people were also meant to develop a rational state of consciousness whereby they would come to understand and accept that the answer to prayer would always be guided by the laws of God, such as the Law of Free Will and the Law of Cause and Effect.

People must now rise above that state of consciousness. In the past, people perceived God as being separate from themselves, meaning that they saw God as being "up there." People must overcome that sense of separation from God. People must begin to see God as being inside themselves, as being "in here" instead of "out there." When you understand that you are a co-creator with God, you realize that God is not some kind of genie who will answer your every request and do all the work for you. You realize that God will answer your prayer, but it is not likely to happen in the form of a miracle. God will answer your prayer through you and your own efforts, as long as those efforts make use of God's laws. The way to have your prayers answered is to know the laws that God used to create the universe. You must learn to use those laws to co-create the universe that you desire to experience.

When you begin to develop Christ consciousness, you come to the realization expressed in my saying: "I can of my own self do nothing" (John 5:30). When you are caught in the death consciousness, you think you are the doer, and you do not realize that you can only act by using God's energy. When you escape the death consciousness, you realize that the outer mind, the outer person, can do nothing of its own power. It can act only by using God's energy which comes from within. As you begin to identify yourself as a Christed being, you come to the realization expressed in my saying: "My Father worketh hitherto, and I work" (John 5:17). You realize that God has created a foundation, and you must now build upon it. You are not a puppet on a string; God is working through you. When you attain Christ consciousness, you see that everything you do is a collaborative effort between you and God, between your Conscious You and your spiritual self. Your Conscious You is not a robot; it is a natural extension of your I AM Presence. Your spiritual self is the anchor for your God-given individuality, and you are expressing that individuality through your soul vehicle. Your lifestream is choosing how to express your individuality in this world.

When you reach this level of awareness, you gain an entirely different perspective on prayer. You no longer see God as an external entity – as a genie in a bottle – who will magically answer your every request. You see yourself as being an extension of God, and therefore God is acting through you. God is not answering your prayer *for* you. God is answering your prayer *through* you. Your prayer no longer takes the form of a request; it takes the form of a visualization and an affirmation of what you want to see manifest. Just read the scriptures and learn from my absolute certainty that God would manifest what I accepted as already mine.

You do not make the prayer with the consciousness that you don't have what you are asking for. You make the prayer with the consciousness that what you desire is already manifest in the spiritual world; you simply need to use God's laws to bring it into the material world. I have tried to explain that everything is created through the mind of a conscious being. God must bring things into the material world through your consciousness. When you are a co-creator with God, you are not passively waiting for God to answer your prayer. You are actively working with God to bring into manifestation that which you desire.

In summary, one might say that if all of your prayers were answered by an external God, you might never begin to co-create with the internal God.

**You seem to be saying that difficult situations are often the result of karma from past lives. I realize your whole point for telling us this is to show us that we don't have to be the slaves of that karma but that we can take active measures to overcome it. Yet I think many people feel like this can be an overwhelming task. I have known people who started the spiritual path with great enthusiasm and then gave up because it seemed like they were getting nowhere. What would you say to help people avoid becoming discouraged and giving up on the path?**

It is helpful to understand that the purpose of life is not just to pay back your karma. Even when a lifestream pays back its debts to life and resolves all erroneous beliefs, it still might not be ready to permanently ascend to the spiritual realm. To understand this, you need to talk about two phases of the lifestream's growth. When we talk about paying back your debts to life, we are talking about a lifestream who has fallen or descended into a lower state of consciousness. The lifestream has misqualified energy, or it would have no debt to life. The misqualified energy creates a gravitational pull that keeps the lifestream tied to the material universe. The lifestream cannot ascend back to the spiritual realm until the karma is balanced. One might say that the lifestream's karma acts as a rubber band that pulls it back to earth.

When we talk about the need for salvation, we talk about the need for the lifestream to be free of the conditions created after it fell into a lower state of consciousness. It is essential to remember that when the lifestream first made the choice to descend to earth, it did not plan on making karma, misqualifying energy or accepting beliefs that are out of touch with the reality of God. When the lifestream decided to descend to earth, it had a positive purpose for coming here. Before the lifestream can permanently leave the earth behind, it must fulfill that purpose. A lifestream might have one or all of the following reasons for wanting to descend to earth:

• The lifestream might have a legitimate desire to experience life at this level of God's creation.

• The lifestream might have a legitimate desire to express itself through a physical body.

• The lifestream might desire to express its God-given individuality in the material world.

• The lifestream might desire to bring the light of God into the material universe and, by expressing its individuality, serve as a co-creator who helps bring God's kingdom to earth.

• After a number of lifestreams fell, other lifestreams chose to descend to earth on a rescue mission to bring fallen lifestreams back home.

Every lifestream originally had a purpose, one might call it a divine plan, for wanting to descend to earth. As long as that divine plan has not been fulfilled, the lifestream is not free to ascend back to the spiritual realm. The lifestream does not want to come back to the spiritual realm because it feels that it still has an unfulfilled mission on earth. Even if a lifestream pays back all of its debts to life, it will not automatically ascend back to Heaven. The lifestream must fulfill its reason for coming here so that it can voluntarily choose to leave the earth behind and ascend to the spiritual world. God will never force the lifestream to ascend; it must be a free choice. However, until you have balanced your karma, you don't have the option to ascend.

When a lifestream falls into the death consciousness, and begins to accumulate misqualified energy and erroneous beliefs, it might forget its original purpose for coming here. Many lifestreams on earth are currently so burdened by their personal karma and erroneous beliefs that they have forgotten all about a higher purpose to life. They are simply struggling to survive, and they go from one crisis to the next. As the lifestream begins the process of removing the misqualified energy and overcoming its erroneous beliefs, it will, so to speak, get its head above the water. Instead of feeling like it is drowning in a sea of misqualified energy, it can now catch its breath and start looking around. Hopefully, the lifestream will discover the rock of Christ – meaning the spiritual path – and decide to swim for that rock.

As the lifestream moves forward on the spiritual path, it can begin to spend less time and energy balancing karma and more time and energy fulfilling its positive desires and goals. If you will diligently apply yourself to the spiritual path and do the hard and unpleasant work of removing karma and overcoming erroneous beliefs, you will eventually reach a breakthrough point. Once you pass that point, the path no longer seems like such hard work. You no longer feel like you are stuck in the mud and getting nowhere. Instead, you begin to work on positive goals and realize that life is not a treadmill. Life is a wonderful opportunity to express your God-given individuality and help make the world a better place.

My heart truly goes out to the millions of people who are currently so burdened by their personal karma and psychology that they have no attention left over for wondering about the purpose of life. I truly wish there was a way to reach these lifestreams and make them engage in the spiritual path that would lead them to the breakthrough point.

Obviously, I want to see all lifestreams come home to God. But my more immediate desire is to see all lifestreams go beyond the breakthrough point so that they can begin to approach life as a positive experience rather than some form of punishment forced upon them by an angry God or a mindless machine. I desire to help every person realize that there is a systematic path to personal salvation. I want to see every lifestream recognize that path, anchor itself firmly on that path and pass the breakthrough point.

I wish all people could feel my passion and my all-consuming desire to help them reach that breakthrough point and come to see life as a wonderful opportunity, a wonderful gift from God. I had that desire when I walked the earth 2,000 years ago. That is why I had such compassion for the downtrodden and the afflicted who were weighted down by their own karma and their limited beliefs. My desire has only grown stronger since then.

This is the message that I wanted my disciples to shout from the housetops. I wanted them to shout: "Life doesn't have to be this way. Life doesn't have to be a struggle. It is your own sense of struggle that creates the struggle. The kingdom of God is at hand. The kingdom of God is within you. It is a higher state of consciousness, and there is a systematic path that leads you to that state of consciousness. All you have to do is recognize the existence of the path and decide that you are willing to put one foot in front of the other. As long as you keep taking one step at a time, you will reach the breakthrough point. You will come up higher in consciousness. You will realize and accept that life is a wonderful gift from God, and you will have the abundant life. I have walked that path. Come follow me into the glory and the joy of God. I am the Good Shepherd and I am here to call you home!"

**That describes my own experience. I remember struggling for years, feeling like the spiritual path was just hard work and wondering if I was making any progress at all. Then, I suddenly reached the breakthrough point, and although there is still work to be done, it is so much more enjoyable. I too wish all people could reach that breakthrough point.**

That desire is shared by every ascended being. God never wanted people to be burdened by their misqualified energy and their limited beliefs. God never wanted people to lose contact with the spiritual realm, to lose hope or to feel that life is a meaningless struggle against forces beyond their control. God never wanted this situation and God would love to see it changed as quickly as possible.

The reason you recognize your own experience in my description is that this is a universal path that all people must follow. Every person who has ever attained spiritual mastery has followed that same path of reaching for a higher state of consciousness. Because people have turned me into an idol, they rarely consider that I too walked the path. I had to go through the same struggle that every human being on earth is currently going through. I know what it is like to be on earth. I descended to earth and I fell into the death consciousness. I misqualified energy and I accepted limited beliefs. I had to walk a systematic path to overcome those conditions and get back to a higher state of consciousness.

My real breakthrough into the higher state of consciousness came during my 40 days in the desert. It was then that I began to realize my true identity as a spiritual being. That realization enabled me to start my mission as Jesus Christ. My plea to all people is to accept me, Jesus Christ, as your older brother. I am in no way above or apart from you. I walked the same path that you are walking. I fought the same battles that you are fighting. I faced the same challenges that you are facing. I fought my way through the jungle of the lower state of consciousness, and if you will accept me as an example, you can follow in my footsteps.

The only reason I came to earth was to set forth an example for all to follow. Please dare to follow that example. Please accept that you are worthy and capable of following my example. If you will do this, you will one day reach the gate that leads to the spiritual world. I promise you that I will be there to meet you with open arms and a heart that overflows with a love so tender that it is beyond your present imagination.

Before I ascended, I said: "And I, if I be lifted up from the earth, will draw all men unto me" (John 12:32). What will draw all people unto me is the love of my Sacred Heart that I am constantly pouring out to anyone who is willing to open his or her heart and accept my love. Please let me into your heart. Please let my love into your heart, and let it form a magnet that will draw you back into the spiritual kingdom where you truly belong.

## 11 | RISE ABOVE GUILT

**We have talked about the need to come apart from the mass consciousness, and in my opinion one aspect of this consciousness is the idea that we are all sinners and that we should feel guilty for being alive. I understand that we need to admit our mistakes so we can learn how to stop repeating them. Yet once we overcome a tendency to make a certain mistake, is there any reason to feel guilty? Is guilt really a necessary part of spiritual growth and will it help us come closer to Christ consciousness?**

I earlier talked about people who have descended far below the level of the Christ consciousness and have not yet turned around. For such people guilt can be a necessary part of the awakening that helps them stop descending further down the staircase. Some lifestreams have actually turned around and started the uphill path as a result of feeling guilty. Unfortunately, many other lifestreams have been taken into a blind alley by guilt. They feel so guilty that they dare not rise above a certain level on the spiritual path. Obviously, this is not what I want to see happen.

I would very much prefer that all people could be turned around through a greater awareness of the spiritual reality instead of being turned around through a crisis that leads to guilt, fear or other negative emotions. I think it should be obvious that you cannot take such negative emotions with you into Heaven. The ascended masters never feel guilt, fear or any other human emotions. After all, if you feel guilty, you are not responding to the situation with love—you are not loving yourself. As you ascend the spiritual path, you will have to overcome all sense of guilt and all tendency to blame yourself or accept blame from the world. Guilt is definitely a frame of mind that must be left behind on the path to Christhood.

**If we are to leave behind guilt, I think we need to talk about the fact that some religions – Christianity being a prime example – make it sound like we were conceived in sin and anything we do is sinful. What would you say to that?**

The I AM Presence of every human being was created by a set of spiritual parents. These parents reside in the spiritual world, and they are perfectly attuned to the vision and the perfection of God. When spiritual beings create a new I AM Presence, they use their creative abilities within the framework of God's vision and God's law. Consequently, the I AM Presence of every human being was created to be perfect.

Your Conscious You was created by your I AM Presence, and it was also created to express the perfection of God. Your Conscious You was created from the higher energies of the spiritual realm. Yet, as mandated by God's law, every Conscious You was given the gift of free will. The Conscious

You can choose to move away from the original perfection envisioned by its spiritual parents. This does not happen in an instant but over many lifetimes. A Conscious You can gradually move so far away from its original purity that it loses conscious awareness of its true identity. The Conscious You no longer sees itself as a perfect being created by spiritual parents. Instead, it sees itself as an imperfect, mortal, human being, and it has no idea from where it came.

Because the universe is a mirror, you will create according to the contents of your consciousness. If you see yourself as imperfect or limited, you will create imperfections and limitations—and the universe will mirror this back to you. However, no matter how far you have descended into imperfection, nothing you have ever done has erased or degraded the original purity of your being. No matter what the surface appearances might be, deep within your being is the original blueprint, or matrix, created by your spiritual parents. The original blueprint is like a pearl that is covered over by layers of dirt. If you will make an effort to wash away the dirt, you can uncover the pearl of your being, the pearl of great price (Matthew 13:46).

No matter how imperfect the outer appearances may be – on the planet as a whole or in the life and consciousness of an individual – nothing can destroy the Conscious You's potential to turn around and move back to God and its original identity. Every Conscious You has that potential. There is absolutely no force in this world that can take away your potential to come back to God. There are numerous forces in this world who claim to have this power. These forces are constantly seeking to convince human beings that there is nothing they could personally do to come back to God.

Incidentally, some of these forces claim to be representatives of God and they have managed to take high positions in some religions. As I have said numerous times, everything revolves around your free will. No matter what the forces of this world might say, the fact remains that you can begin a systematic path that leads you back to God. Nothing can stop you from following that path—except your own decision to accept that you are unworthy or incapable of approaching God. If you allow someone to convince you that you are a miserable sinner who will be rejected by God, then God must respect that decision. However, if you allow me, or any other true spiritual teacher, to inspire you to understand and know the unconditional love of God, you can begin the path that leads you out of imperfection and back into the light and the love of God.

If a sufficient number of human beings will walk the path, the entire planet will be raised out of the current state of misery and imperfection. It can literally be raised into the perfection of God, and thereby the kingdom of God will come into full physical manifestation on this planet. How can the kingdom of God be brought to this planet? It can be brought only through the minds of those who are meant to be co-creators. God will not suddenly appear in the sky and whisk away all the problems and imperfections created by human beings. Doing so would violate people's free will and their right to learn by reaping the consequences of their actions. God does not violate his own laws. God's kingdom can be brought only if human beings accept their spiritual identity and their potential to co-create with God. People can then begin to co-create divine perfection instead of the human imperfection currently seen on this planet.

My basic answer is that no matter what anyone says, nothing on this planet is inherently sinful or imperfect. Everything on this planet was created from the pure light of God. The light of God can never be fundamentally altered. Let me return to my analogy of a movie projector. The light bulb in the projector produces a constant stream of white light. As the white light passes through the filmstrip, it is colored by the images on the filmstrip, and those images are projected onto the movie screen. However, the white light has not been fundamentally altered, and the images are not permanently burned onto the movie screen. To change the images that appear on the movie screen, you simply need to change the images on the filmstrip.

Imagine yourself in a movie theater, watching a horror movie. The images are only temporarily projected upon the screen. At any moment, you can change the filmstrip and you will instantly have new images projected upon the same screen that only a moment ago showed the horror movie. Currently, the screen of life, which human beings call planet earth, is projecting an imperfect image. Yet if a sufficient number of human beings will make an effort to change the filmstrip inside their own minds, the planet will gradually begin to project a more beautiful image. Because of the density of the material universe, the change will not be instantaneous. It will be a gradual change, but if a sufficient number of people raise their consciousness, you will begin to see swift progress. There is a potential for bringing positive changes that are so dramatic that most people simply cannot conceive of or believe that such changes could occur.

Do not let those who are trapped in the lower state of consciousness make you believe that this planet is doomed or going to hell in a hand basket. Nothing is set in stone. Nothing is predestined. The biggest lie promoted by those who are working against God's purposes is that once you have crossed a certain line, there is no turning back. Once you have sinned, there is no way for you to save yourself.

This is a malicious lie. It is completely and utterly out of touch with the reality of God. There is absolutely no state of imperfection that cannot be transformed back to its original God-purity. When you watch a movie, the permanent elements are the light streaming through the projector and the movie screen itself. These elements remain the same no matter which movie is currently shown in the theater. Regardless of what images appear on the screen, the white light and the white screen remain unchanged.

Regardless of the current imperfect images appearing on planet earth, the basic elements of God's creation are completely and utterly unchanged. To change the temporary images, you simply need to change the filmstrip. That filmstrip is located in the minds of human beings.

Change the filmstrip and you will change what appears on the screen of life on planet earth. I realize this is a message that many people will find it difficult to accept. Yet it is the simple and basic truth about life. The situation on planet earth is a movie projected upon the screen of life. Currently, it is a horror movie. Yet if you will change the filmstrip, you can change the movie into the most beautiful inspirational movie you can possibly imagine. Whatever you imagine is what will be projected onto the screen. If you want to change your outer reality, begin by changing your inner perception of "reality."

**You make it sound so simple and easy.**

That is because I want people to understand the basic process, and the basic process really is quite simple. The material universe is literally an image projected onto the screen of God's consciousness, projected into the cosmic mirror. There is nothing complicated about it; it is only the duality of the death consciousness that makes it seem complicated and overwhelming. Don't forget that I have been in embodiment on this planet. I fully realize that everything looks different when you see it from inside the box of the death consciousness. However, there is a fundamental difference between feeling trapped inside that box (or feeling like there is nothing outside the box) and realizing that there is a viable and systematic path that leads you out of the box.

Once you realize and accept that there is a way out, you gain an entirely new perspective on life. You are filled with a new hope, a new sense of direction and purpose. You realize that life really does make sense. It was only the duality of the egoic mind (and doctrines springing from that duality) that made it seem like things didn't make sense. You realize that if an outer doctrine cannot answer your questions, you can simply look beyond that doctrine and find answers from a higher source. You realize that God has created a logical and orderly universe and that there is a way out of the misery of the lower state of consciousness.

A lifestream might have spent many lifetimes moving away from God and thereby sinking deeper and deeper into the lower state of consciousness. Yet every lifestream has the potential to rise above it. Will it take work? Yes it will, and that is why I said: "In your patience posses ye your souls" (Luke 21:19). That is why I talk about a systematic and gradual path. The path has many levels and it cannot be completed in an instant. However, most people are already walking the path, they are simply not consciously aware of it. Most lifestreams have already made tremendous progress, and if they will come to a conscious realization of the path, they can make more rapid progress.

Millions of lifestreams have the potential to rise out of the death consciousness in the remainder of this lifetime. If they will make a conscious effort to do so, they will help bring God's kingdom to earth—in this lifetime.

**That is quite a promise, but I have to say that I know people who aren't interested in God's kingdom**

**because they think it will take away their freedom and creativity.**

I am aware of this, and I fully understand why so many people feel that way. However, let us be honest and recognize that this idea springs from the image of God that has been portrayed by so many orthodox religions. These religions have painted an image of God as an angry and judgmental deity who is ready to punish anyone for stepping outside of his law and his will. As I explain in *The Mystical Teachings of Jesus*, this image is out of touch with the reality of God.

God is a God of love, and God has given you the imagination and the free will that is the basis for your creative expression. Your spiritual parents want you to use your creativity in ways that are surprising to them. However, they don't want you to use your creativity in ways that are destructive to yourself and your spiritual brothers and sisters. One of the main problems in this context is that so many people tend to think the words "perfection" and "God's kingdom" describe something that is static. The duality of the death consciousness makes people think that if something is perfect, it could not possibly change. This is an incorrect definition of the concept of perfection.

Perfection means something that is in harmony with God's law. When a human being attains Christ consciousness that person literally becomes perfect according to the true definition of perfection. This does not mean that the person loses all individuality or creativity. On the contrary, the person gains the true individuality that is anchored in his or her I AM Presence. The person attains the unlimited creativity that springs from your God-given individuality.

Your Conscious You was designed to be a co-creator with God. Let us compare this to building an elaborate castle. The spiritual being that most people call God simply acts as a structural engineer. God has defined natural laws which insure that the castle will not collapse. However, God has not created a static design of the castle. As long as the design follows the basic structural laws so that it will not self-destruct, God allows the artisans, namely spiritual and human beings, to design the castle according to their creative vision.

Both materialistic scientists and orthodox religious people cling to the idea that everything in this world is predetermined. This is a false idea that springs from the death consciousness. Nothing is predetermined because everything is subject to the free will of both spiritual and human beings. God has not created a blueprint that is set in stone. God has created a foundation and expects human beings to act as co-creators and build a castle upon his foundation. The design of the castle is not predetermined in every detail. It is literally up to human beings to design many aspects of the castle according to their imagination and vision. God wants to be surprised by the creativity of his sons and daughters. That is the inner meaning of my statement: "My Father worketh hitherto, and I work" (John 5:17). When you attain the Christ consciousness, you see that God has created a set of perfect laws that do not restrict but enhance your creativity. You can then begin to build upon that foundation and fill your rightful role as a co-creator with God.

Human beings need to use their creative abilities in harmony with the basic laws set up to ensure that the material universe will not self-destruct. Staying within the framework of these laws still gives you unlimited opportunity for creative expression. As long as your creation follows the basic laws defined by God, it will be perfect. However, there are millions of ways to create something perfect.

If human beings create outside of the laws of God, their creation will be imperfect. This does not mean that God will instantly punish human beings for their mistakes. It simply means that the impersonal laws created by God will cause people's creation to self-destruct. One of the basic laws discovered by science is the second law of thermodynamics. This law states that in a closed system disorder will increase and all structures will eventually break down.

This law actually demonstrates that when you cut yourself off from God, everything you create will break down and self-destruct. In reality, cutting yourself off from God means descending into the death consciousness. When people descend into duality, they become subject to the second law of thermodynamics and so does most of what people have created on this planet. The lower consciousness has even influenced nature, and that is why you see so much decay on planet earth. We explain this in great detail in *Healing Mother Earth*.

To avoid cutting yourself off from God, you must reach beyond the death consciousness and attain some measure of Christ consciousness. The essence of Christ consciousness is that you have a direct connection to the spiritual realm. Through that connection, you can know the laws of God and thereby create within the context of those laws. As a result, your creation will not be subject to the second law of thermodynamics and it will not self-destruct. You can create true and lasting beauty on this planet. You can create the kingdom of God which will evolve forever without breaking down, in contrast to the current kingdom of man which is created in imperfection.

**Since we were created by God, it seems like the idea of sin, especially the concept of original sin, has been somewhat misconstrued. What is your explanation of sin?**

The correct translation of the Hebrew word for "sin" is "missing the mark." Let us relate that to what we just talked about. If you create something that is in harmony with the laws of God, your creation is perfect, meaning that it hits the mark. If your creation violates the laws of God, you are missing the mark.

To sin means that you are missing the mark of creating in harmony with God's laws. It is important for people to realize that when a lifestream is created that lifestream can be compared to a child. God does not expect a young lifestream to instantly know all of his laws. God expects that the lifestream will go through a growth process whereby it gradually learns the laws of God and how to create within the context of those laws. God does not expect people to be perfect – according to a human standard – and therefore God does not condemn people for making mistakes.

However, God also expects people to learn from their mistakes so that they do not keep repeating the same mistakes in an endless cycle that causes them to descend further and further into the death consciousness. From God's perspective there is no association between sin and guilt.

Imagine a child in the process of learning how to walk. What kind of parent would condemn the child for falling down? What kind of parent wants the child to feel guilty for not being able to walk right away? What kind of parent wants the child to feel like a miserable sinner who never dares to take another step? Well, if human parents do not condemn their children for not being able to walk right away, why do these human beings imagine that their heavenly parents would condemn them for missing the mark on the first try? Why do people fail to see that God allows them time to grow and that God does not condemn them for making mistakes?

Obviously, God wants to see you grow and learn your lessons in life so that you can quickly attain a state of consciousness in which you can always hit the mark and create in harmony with God's laws. God does not want to see lifestreams who keep repeating the same mistakes and out of fear, guilt or pride do not want to recognize their mistakes and learn to do better. God does not want people to hold themselves back and prevent themselves from learning the lessons of life. However, even when people do keep repeating the same mistakes, God does not condemn them.

The most important thing to understand about sin is that from God's perspective there is no connection between sin and guilt, blame or condemnation, including self-condemnation. God does not want you to condemn yourself for missing the mark. God wants you to learn your lesson and do better the next time you try. Committing a sin simply means that you missed the mark, and therefore your creation is not fully in harmony with the laws of God. Do not condemn yourself or feel that you are not worthy to try again. Simply learn from your mistake and immediately try again so that you can do better the next time. It is much like falling off a horse. You have to get right back on.

### How did the concept of original sin enter the picture? Does it have any foundation in reality?

That is a complex question. The current explanation of original sin is out of touch with reality, but the concept itself does have a foundation in reality. To understand this, let us make it clear that the concept of original sin does not apply to the Conscious You. The Conscious You was created by the spiritual self who knows the laws of God. The Conscious You of every human being was created in perfection. If a Conscious You was created in harmony with the laws of God, then obviously it could not have been created in sin. The Conscious You could not be created to sin, and therefore the concept of original sin has no bearing on the Conscious You.

Because most people have descended into the death consciousness, they have lost the vision of the original purity of their conscious selves. Most people do not identify themselves as spiritual beings created in God's image and likeness. They have built a new sense of identity influenced by the imperfections they see in the world and in their physical bodies. Millions of people identify themselves as a physical body and nothing more.

When the earth was created, the planet, including the human body, expressed the perfection and purity of God. Over a long period of time, human beings have caused the original blueprint for planet earth to be polluted and thereby altered according to the imperfections of the lower consciousness. This also applies to the human body. The physical bodies that people are currently wearing do not express the perfection of God. That is why you see so many diseases and other imperfections and infirmities.

Some scientists are already aware that information plays a critical role in the creation of the material universe. Through the power of their minds, people impose an image upon the pure light of God. One might say that the universe is created from energy and that information causes the energy to take on a particular form. That information must be conceived by a conscious mind.

Most people are aware that the physical body is designed according to information that is stored in the genes, the DNA. What most scientists have not yet realized or acknowledged is that some of the information stored in DNA originated in the human mind. The human mind imposes information on the DNA molecules so that the physical body itself is influenced by consciousness.

To avoid going into a long technical discussion, let me get back to my original point. When a physical body is conceived, the information stored in the DNA of the parents is combined to form the blueprint for the body of the child. If both parents have descended into the death consciousness, the information in their DNA will be a reflection of that lower state of consciousness. The body they conceive will not be in alignment with the perfect blueprint for a physical body. The blueprint for the child's body will miss the mark. One can say that the child was conceived and born in sin.

The concept of original sin has a basis in reality. When the parents are trapped in the death consciousness, their children will be conceived in sin, meaning that their bodies will not be an expression of the perfection of God. From the beginning, the blueprint of the child's body misses the mark of God's perfection. Take note that this does not mean that a physical body is inherently imperfect or full of sin. God created perfect bodies, and when people raise their consciousness, their bodies will once again express that perfection. Because the body is not inherently sinful, the concept of original sin refers to a temporary phenomenon.

Let me make it clear that the concept of original sin does not refer to the act of sexual intercourse. There is nothing inherently sinful in the physical union between a man and a woman. What can make this act sinful, meaning that the act misses the mark, is the state of consciousness with which the act is performed. This is the case for any other act performed by human beings. If an act is performed from the death consciousness, it will miss the mark. If that same act is performed with a measure of Christ consciousness, it will hit the mark. Obviously, I am not thereby saying that if you kill another person from a state of Christ consciousness, you will not commit a sin. When you have attained Christ consciousness, you would never consider killing another human being.

Sin is not simply a matter of outer actions. Certain actions are always sinful. However, many actions are sinful only when performed from the lower consciousness. Yet these same actions can be performed with a measure of Christ consciousness, and therefore they will not be sinful. I understand that this is a subtle and difficult distinction, and I am fully aware that many people will reject this entire idea. Many people look at everything in terms of black and white. They want to have a set of simple rules, saying that this act is always sinful and that act is always good.

God did not design this universe based on the death consciousness. No matter what seems convenient to that state of consciousness, the reality of God remains unchanged. You cannot determine whether an act is sinful by using the relativity of the human ego. You can determine whether an act is sinful only by using the higher standard of the Christ mind.

**I understand what you are saying about learning from our mistakes and not blaming ourselves. Yet what about people who have committed very severe mistakes that might have caused the death of another human being. For example, I have met several women who still feel guilty for having had an abortion many years ago. How can people overcome the guilt and grief of having made a severe mistake?**

Let me give you a teaching that applies to any human being and any type of mistake—I will simply use abortion as an example. The first thing you need to do is to fully recognize that you have made a mistake. I realize that this represents somewhat of a Catch-22. If you admit that you made a mistake, you will automatically feel guilty so it is safer not to admit your mistakes and instead seek to justify your actions. Human beings are exceptionally good at not taking responsibility for their mistakes. Yet if you are a true spiritual seeker, you cannot allow yourself to fall into this trap.

Any mistake you could possibly make is a product of a limited state of consciousness. The only way to rise above that frame of mind is to admit your mistake, see it for what it is and choose to leave it behind. When you truly understand the following teaching, admitting your mistakes will not cause you to become trapped in guilt—even if they are severe mistakes. You will simply learn from those mistakes, make the choice to leave the limited consciousness behind and then move a step closer to Christhood.

Once you have admitted your mistake, you need to accept that God loves you with a love that is unconditional, and therefore he has already forgiven you! What stands in the way of you experiencing that forgiveness is your own lack of acceptance of God's forgiveness. You need to accept that God has forgiven you and I, Jesus Christ, have forgiven you. What is left is that you need to forgive yourself. I realize that telling people to forgive themselves is almost like telling a blind man to open his eyes and see. Yet the truth shall make you free so let me give you some thoughts to ponder that might indeed help you forgive yourself.

There is a force in this world that is consumed by a desire to prove God wrong, to prove that God made a mistake when he gave human beings free will. This force, which is actually a state of consciousness, will do anything possible to cause people to misuse their free will so that they separate themselves from God. As mentioned earlier, when God gave lifestreams free will, he had to give them the ability to violate his laws—otherwise they would not truly have free will. By giving them this opportunity, God was hoping that, as lifestreams experimented with their free will, they would gradually come to the realization that it was in their own best interest, and indeed it was their highest love, to help co-create the universe within the framework of God's overall vision and plan. Indeed, God was hoping that, after sending lifestreams into the world of form, they would – of their own free will – choose to build a sense of oneness with God.

The foremost goal of the forces who are working against God's plan is to cause people to separate themselves from God and to become stuck in a state of consciousness in which they see themselves as separated from God. This has caused these forces to set up numerous traps on planet earth. These traps have the overall purpose of causing people to see themselves as separated from God. A great number of these traps have the purpose of causing people to violate God's laws. This is done by creating an almost unlimited number of serpentine lies that make it seem like it is necessary, justified or acceptable to violate God's laws.

It is precisely this state of consciousness that is the hidden force behind all of the atrocities you see on this planet. The strategy is to create a mindset which entices people to believe that they have a right to decide their own destiny and that, in order to decide for themselves, they can commit this or that act. One of the many subtle arguments used by dark forces is that an unborn child is nothing but a blob of tissue. Yet many of the women who have had an abortion have experienced various levels of grief, remorse and a sense of loss. This very fact should prove beyond any doubt that an unborn child is not a blob of tissue, and that is why a sensitive woman will know that her abortion took away the opportunity for a lifestream to come into embodiment. Can you see the subtle plot here? Even though there are many dark intentions involved in the abortion issue, the overall intention is to fool women into taking the life of an unborn child out of ignorance or insensitivity. Let us now consider what happens to a woman who has had an abortion. There are two basic reactions.

I can assure you that every woman who has an abortion will experience a moment of truth in which she realizes that she made a mistake. There are, however, many women who barely notice this moment of truth or who push it aside so quickly that they claim they cannot even remember it. Yet I can assure you that a bit of honest soul searching would reveal to any woman that she did have a moment of truth before or after having an abortion. This is the same for any mistake a person could possibly make. There is always a moment of truth.

When a woman denies the moment of truth, she can do so only by adopting a mindset of insensitivity to life. She can do so only by denying her connection to the unborn child in her womb. She can deny this connection only by denying her connection to all life, and especially to the divine mother herself. By denying her connection to life, a woman has set herself apart from God. She thinks she is separated from God, and therefore she is separated from all life. That is why she can deny the idea that an abortion takes life.

When a woman adopts this reaction, the dark forces have won because she has separated herself out from God. In many cases, a woman will go to great length to defend her decision to have the abortion and thereby cement the sense of being separated from God. She might even go to great length to try to convince other people that an abortion is okay, and thereby cause such people to also see themselves as separated from God. She is simply perpetuating the serpentine lie that caused her to make the mistake in the first place.

Now let us look at the second scenario, namely that of a
woman who chooses to acknowledge and admit the moment
of truth. This woman realizes and admits that she made a mistake, which gives her the opportunity to become free of the
serpentine lie and the dark forces. Obviously, a woman can
make this decision only if she acknowledges a certain connection to life. By acknowledging this connection, the woman is
also acknowledging her connection to God. Obviously, this is
the exact opposite of what the dark forces want. However, this
does not mean that they have lost the battle for the woman's
soul. It only means that the dark forces now go to Plan B.

The primary plan of the dark forces is to get people to
deny their connection to God and thereby deny that they ever
made a mistake. If the dark forces cannot prevent people from
acknowledging that they made a mistake, they will use the next
plot in their strategy. That plot is to give the person such a
sense of guilt, such a sense of being a sinner, that the person
feels that he or she can never again make things right with
God.

When it comes to a woman having an abortion, the dark
forces will project into your mind and emotional body the
thought and feeling that you have committed such a grave
mistake that you could never, ever make up for it. They will
do this in a deliberate attempt to make you feel that you can
never again be acceptable in the eyes of God, thereby causing
you to separate yourself out from God by feeling that you are
unworthy to be connected to God. They are trying to make
sure that even though you have admitted making a mistake,
you will never be free of that mistake.

The first plan is to manipulate people into making a mistake and deny that they made a mistake. Thereby, people will
never be free of the mistake in the sense that they are trapped
in the consciousness that caused them to make the mistake.

If that plan doesn't work – because people do admit that they made a mistake – the dark forces will attempt to make sure that you feel such guilt over having made a mistake that you still will not be free of the mistake. They will do this by making you feel that you could never be redeemed for that mistake. The plot here is to trick you into making a mistake by violating God's laws and then try to trick you into never being free of the mistake or the consciousness, the serpentine lie, behind it. The dark forces are seeking to manipulate people into a spiritual catch-22.

Consider how subtle and how sinister this plot is. Billions of people have been tricked by this plot and its numerous variations. This was never God's plan when he gave his sons and daughters free will. God has no desire to see people become lost in a state of consciousness in which they deny their oneness with him. He has only one desire and that is to see you recognize the fullness of who you are as a son or daughter of God who has the potential to be one with God, to be a co-creator with God and to be God in this material universe. God never desired you to fall into a lower state of consciousness in which you see yourself as separated from him. Once you have fallen into the death consciousness, God has only one desire and that is to see you rise out of that state of consciousness and accept your true identity as a son or daughter who is blameless before God.

When God gave you free will, he gave you the right to experiment within the framework of the natural laws that are upholding the universe. Because energy is a form of vibration, it can be easily changed. The material universe is literally like a cosmic sandbox in which you have a right to build any castle you like. Some castles will not be the best possible. However, you have not changed the sand; you have simply given it an undesirable form. To erase your mistake, just break down the  castle and build a better one.

When you make an imperfect choice and violate God's law, you are lowering the vibration of a portion of God's energy. You do this through the power of your mind. Yet the very fact that your mind has the power to lower the vibration of God's energy should prove to you that your mind also has the power to raise the vibration of God's energy. There is no mistake you could possibly make in this universe that could not be erased completely. A mistake is simply misqualified energy, and once you raise the vibration of that energy, your mistake is erased permanently. It is not possible for a human being to make a mistake that is permanent. Anything you do in this temporary universe will be a temporary manifestation, and therefore it can be erased.

If you make a mistake, God does not want you to feel guilty over having made a mistake. God wants you to recognize and admit that you made a mistake and then learn the lesson of how to make better choices in the future. This means that you must learn to see through and forsake the serpentine lie that caused you to make the mistake—even the entire dualistic state of mind that causes you to be vulnerable to the serpentine lies. Once you have learned that lesson and truly forsaken the belief or consciousness that caused you to make the mistake, there is no constructive purpose for feeling guilty over having made a mistake. God gave you free will. God gave you the right to experiment with that free will, even to the point of violating the laws of nature. God did this because he wanted you to have the opportunity to learn that following God's law is in your own best interest and is what the Conscious You loves most. God does not want you to feel guilty; God simply wants you to move on and learn your lesson from making a mistake so that you can come up higher in consciousness.

The dark forces are attempting to trap you in a state of consciousness that causes you to see yourself as separate from God. As one way to do this, they have created the entire consciousness of sin and guilt. The belief that you could never be redeemed for having made a mistake or committed a sin did not come from God, and it is distinctly anti-christ in nature. One of the most important messages behind my coming to earth was that human beings can be redeemed and can be completely free from any mistakes they have made here on earth. You can be as free from these mistakes as if the mistakes had never happened. Unfortunately, many people have fallen prey to the serpentine consciousness, and therefore they think they could never truly be redeemed. This prevents them from accepting God's forgiveness.

Once again, the subtleness of the dark forces is very tricky. If they cannot ensnare you one way, they will seek to ensnare you the other way. This does not mean that people should take it lightly when they make a mistake and simply push it aside as being unimportant. If you do so, you will make more mistakes and therefore become more entrenched in the consciousness that causes you to make mistakes. This consciousness also causes you to lose contact with your spiritual self and to make karma. Everybody needs to be alert to the fact that there are right choices and not so right choices.

When you make a choice that violates the laws of God, you are actually hurting yourself. If people truly understand what they are doing, they will not deliberately hurt themselves. That is why people need to be alert, and they need to evaluate all their choices. They need to constantly seek to expand their understanding – "with all thy getting, get understanding" (Proverbs 4:7) – so that they can know intuitively when they have made an imperfect choice.

Let me sketch the ideal scenario for dealing with a mistake. Whenever you make an imperfect choice, there will always be a moment of truth. Be alert and acknowledge that you made a mistake and seek to gain the best possible understanding of how and why it was a mistake. Learn to see through the serpentine lie behind your mistake. Then decide not to repeat the mistake. Ideally, you should decide to leave behind the consciousness, the lie, that caused you to make that mistake.

When you do this, every mistake you make becomes a stepping stone that brings you closer to Christ consciousness. This is what God wants to see happen for you. This is what I want to see happen for you. I realize that most people have descended into the death consciousness and that they need to follow a gradual path to reach the full Christ consciousness. I have a great desire to see people adopt the right attitude whereby each mistake they make brings them closer to Christ consciousness. In that way, you can only win, and the dark forces have no hold over you. The prince of this world will come and have nothing in you. (John 14:30).

Many people have misunderstood that saying of mine. It does not mean that you have to be perfect or have attained full Christ consciousness before the prince of this world will have nothing in you. It means that you need to adopt the attitude that you are willing to learn from your mistakes and forsake the serpentine lie, the death consciousness, that is the source of all mistakes. You are willing to acknowledge your mistakes without feeling guilty for having made a mistake. You simply learn from the mistake and immediately move higher on your spiritual path. You let a part of your human self die every day, as Paul said (1Corinthians 15:31). You put off the old human, the egoic identity, and put on the Christ mind. When you have this attitude, the devil will have nothing in you whereby he can use your mistake to trick you. You might still have some serpentine beliefs left that will cause you to make other mistakes, but those mistakes also become stepping stones to progress.

Do you see the important point here? I am not saying that it is right to have an abortion or to make other mistakes. I am saying it is a mistake to have an abortion, but it is not a mistake from which you can never escape. You can indeed become free, and the first step is to acknowledge that you made a mistake. The second step is to truly forsake the consciousness that caused you to make the mistake. You truly forsake the wrong belief, the serpentine lie, that caused you to make the mistake. Once you have seen through and forsaken the lie, you must know that, at that very moment, your mistake has been forgiven by God. This understanding brings you to the next step where you need to make a conscious decision to accept God's forgiveness and to simply move on without holding yourself back with a sense of guilt.

After having gone through this inner transformation, you then need to recognize that certain mistakes have consequences that reach beyond your own psyche. If the mistakes affected other parts of life, you will have created a karma in the form of misqualified energy. For you to be truly free of the mistake, the consequences of your actions need to be neutralized. You can compensate for this in various ways, including using a spiritual technique to transmute the karma.

It can take time before you have neutralized the negative consequences, and a sensitive person will know intuitively that he or she has not yet paid back all debt to life for making a certain mistake. This might cause you to hang on to a sense of guilt even though it is not needed. As I have tried to explain, there is no need to feel guilty once you have abandoned the consciousness that caused you to make a mistake. Once you have done so, you need to allow yourself to feel free of guilt. If you are not free of guilt, it shows that you are being attacked by dark forces who are projecting this guilt into your mind and emotional body. As I said earlier, there is much perversion in the emotional body of humankind. It is very easy for the dark forces to use your mistakes to project feelings of guilt into your emotional body.

My advice to all people who have made a mistake for which they think there is no escape is to contemplate the things I have said here. I strongly advise people to use the tools for spiritual protection to call for their minds and emotional bodies to be sealed from all dark forces and their projections of guilt, fear and other negative emotions. You can also call for the judgment of such dark forces, and you should call to Archangel Michael to bind and consume the dark forces attacking you. I also advise you to use Mother Mary's invocations to consume all karma and all misqualified energy resulting from the mistake. *The Miracle Forgiveness Rosary* is a very efficient tool for forgiving yourself.

Finally, I advise people to use the technique for inner attunement [See the book *The Mystical Teachings of Jesus* or *www.transcendencetoolbox.com.*] to gain a deeper understanding of the serpentine lie that caused them to make the mistake. You can also use this technique to give your sense of guilt to me. Simply visualize that you enter the garden and sit down across from me. Then visualize that you take your sense of guilt, or other negative emotions, and cram them into a tight ball. Now visualize that you take that ball and throw it into my Sacred Heart where it is instantly consumed by my unconditional and infinite love. Give this exercise once a day until you feel that you are free of the guilt.

As a closing thought, always keep in mind that you live in a world that is a battleground between two opposing forces. Your soul is the rope between two teams who are engaged in a tug of war. On one side of the rope, you have all of the dark forces out of death and hell, who are pulling on your soul to prevent you from growing. On the other side, you have the ascended masters who are pulling on your Conscious You to come up higher.

However, unlike a normal tug of war, there is no question that one team is infinitely stronger than the other team. We of the ascended masters have the power to pull you up at any moment. The problem is that we have a handicap that often neutralizes our strength. That handicap is the decisions you make as to how you see yourself. If you fall prey to a serpentine lie, such as the lie that you are a miserable sinner who should feel guilty for any mistake you ever made, you will give the other team an unfair advantage that will allow them to pull you down.

Simply decide to learn how to see through the serpentine lies and allow your brothers and sisters of the ascended masters to pull you up higher. Did I not say that if I be lifted up, I would draw all humans unto me (John 12:32)? Do you think I was just kidding? I have the power to pull you into our Father's kingdom—if only you will let me. Simply let go of the guilt that is keeping you tied to the consciousness of hell.

NOTE: This discussion continues in the book *Climbing Higher on the Mystical Path*.

# About the Author

Kim Michaels is an accomplished writer and author. He has conducted spiritual conferences and workshops in 14 countries, has counseled hundreds of spiritual students and has done numerous radio shows on spiritual topics. Kim has been on the spiritual path since 1976. He has studied a wide variety of spiritual teachings and practiced many techniques for raising consciousness. Since 2002 he has served as a messenger for Jesus and other ascended masters. He has brought forth extensive teachings about the mystical path, many of them available for free on his websites: *www.askrealjesus.com*, *www.ascendedmasteranswers.com*, *www.ascendedmasterlight.com* and *www.transcendencetoolbox.com*. For personal information, visit Kim at *www.KimMichaels.info*.

CPSIA information can be obtained
at www.ICGtesting.com
Printed in the USA
LVOW11s1951040517
533197LV00002B/378/P